MW01119214

Life Fulfillment Formula

Formula

120 Ways to Activate Your Potential

Kate Siner PhD

Copyright © 2012 by Kate Siner PhD.

All rights reserved. Printed in the United States of America. Except as permitted under the United States Copyright Act of 1976, no part of this publication may be reproduced or distributed in any form or by any means, or stored in a database or retrieval system, without the prior written permission of the publisher.

ISBN: 0615721028

ISBN-13: 978-0615721026

CONTENTS

INTRODUCTION

Fulfillment is found where the rubber meets the road of life, where we are able to step into our truth — the truth of our existence. That truth that is full and complete. That truth that is eternally flawed. That truth that is magnificent, empowered and utterly human. Where we are willing, also, to accept our inability to do this — or gain humility in our actions. Where we are willing to develop compassion... compassion for ourselves and compassion for others regardless of where they might be on their path. Fulfillment is found where we are able to love deeply and fully and where we have a deep respect for ourselves and others. Fulfillment isn't even necessarily achieving these things — it is simply the willingness to do our best.

There are no free passes. What we put in is what we get. Across the board, that is one truism that seems to stand up regardless of the many perspectives we all navigate. What we need to know at a very deep level is that no exercise in this book will make the slightest bit of difference in our lives if we do not put in the effort. No one but *you* has the ability to save *you*. And, let's not fool ourselves — it is not always easy. Life can be painful and challenging. The truth of our lives can leave us raw and disheartened at times. We can go through parts of our lives that are very dark and very lonely. And, it is still worth it.

With the efforts we put in, the benefits are amazing. We gain the things we have been seeking — love, happiness, success. Situations start to appear differently. What we, at one point, thought was challenge and suffering becomes easy. Where we were once judgmental, we become loving. Where we saw no opportunity there is an *abundance* of opportunity. While we do not get anywhere without effort, we get so much with effort that it can begin to seem effortless. Once we learn that we can help ourselves and others this way, it is clear there is nothing else that we would love more to do.

The reason I wanted to write this book is that I'm tired of people suffering. I am tired of people going through life not knowing that life can be so much different than what they have experienced so far. I know that you are tired of this too. That is why you have chosen your path of growth and that is why you have chosen to help others. I am writing this book for you if you are looking for a way to have a richer, happier, more fulfilled life. I am writing this book because I think that the right tools in the right hands can make a difference in so many people's lives. And, we cannot do it alone. We need the help of others. We need the support of guides.

The Life Fulfillment Formula comes out of my own life experience. At 21, I was pregnant, poor, had a GED and a soon-to-be-deadbeat father of my child. While that is not the beginning of my story, it is a good starting place. It has taken a lot of work just to get to this point. I struggled with depression, anxiety, undiagnosed learning disabilities, and recovery from early childhood trauma. In short, my life was pretty dark and really challenging. What I learned from my own journey — from GED to Ph.D, from pain ridden to deeply fulfilled, from poor to a thriving business person, from disempowered to empowered — is part of what I share with you in this book because I know first-hand that these simple exercises make a profound difference. What I share here in this book also comes from almost 20 years of training, including my Ph.D in Psychology as well as an equal amount of time working directly with people to help them live richer, happier, more fulfilling lives.

At its essence, this book is about becoming a warrior of the heart. It is about becoming fierce and loving. This book is about knowing fear, knowing pain, knowing doubt, and moving forward anyway. This book is about being the person you were meant to be and making the difference you were made to make. It is about teaching others to do the same. It is about helping them see the potential of their lives. It is about learning and teaching that there are simple ways — if you want to put in the effort — to step out of the darkness and open up to new aspects of life.

When most of us look over our lives, we do not see much teaching on how to be fulfilled. Fulfillment comes from our effort to see ourself, be ourself, love ourself, and change ourself. It comes from our effort to connect to the world, to see ourself as part of all things, and to own our responsibility in relationships. Where you have a commitment to see and honor our Connection with all things. What we are often not taught are the simple steps to support this in happening. Fulfillment comes from taking powerful action in the world. Our action is powerful because it comes from our truth and its intention is to be as positive a force as possible. Fulfillment knows that who we are and what we do make a positive difference regardless of whether it is known by millions or only ourselves.

When we work toward fulfillment, we walk toward a life where we make a difference — where we leave a positive mark as the result of having lived. This mark is left on our friends, family and loved ones, our communities, and sometimes our world. When we walk toward fulfillment we walk toward a life with fewer struggles, more joy, and more richness. Even difficult times such as inevitable losses that come with life are filled with a richness that is otherwise not experienced. We leave a legacy for our children or for the children of the world.

The importance of fulfillment is becoming more and more noticed and researched. In the book *The Buddha's Mind,* author Rick Hanson discusses the neuroscience behind experiences such as compassion, fulfillment, and joy. Neuroscience proves that positive emotional and mental experiences can be cultivated so we live a more rewarding live. Steven Covey, in the classic self-improvement book *Seven Habits of Highly Effective People,* shows the real-life improvements that come from developing our character and creating a more positive experience for ourselves. Mohali Csikszentmihalyi, in his book *Flow,* discusses the state where people experience profound enjoyment, creativity, and a complete involvement in life. He proposes that this state can be nurtured as well as spontaneously experienced. The Dalai Lama, in his book *The Art of Happiness*, proposed that the very Purpose of life itself is to seek happiness.

It is clear to me that many of the authors, who use the word "happiness", are using it in a different way than it is most commonly used. I have been hesitant to use the word "happiness" in this book due to what I consider to be the myth of happiness in the American culture. Primarily, this belief goes something like this: I am entitled to happiness and if I am not happy then something is wrong. This is clearly not a true belief. Life has pain as much as it has joy. We are happy at some times and not at others — quite rightly. So, in this book, as some of these other authors on happiness are saying as well, happiness means fulfillment. The sense that life is good and meaningful. I think it is important that we really learn this and that we teach it to others.

This book covers three main areas that are essential to life fulfillment. They are Awareness, Connection and Purpose. Awareness is our understanding of us, our emotions, our thoughts and our actions. It is about learning to work with our shortcomings and develop our strengths. When we do this we see a difference in our relationships, our internal world, and our ability to make a difference. Connection is about how we relate to both others and the world around us. We leave our understanding of the world as separate from us and begin to develop the skills we need to foster health and healing in our relationships. Purpose stands on the shoulders of Awareness. As we become more aware we notice that there is an inner tug that pulls us in a certain direction. When we foster and develop this, we have stepped into our leadership — just by living our lives we make a difference.

What is extremely important is that you do something each day. Walk your talk and help others to do the same. Eventually, you might want to work with a mentor to help you move forward. Join a program where you can be with like-minded people. This will bring you much growth and, ultimately, much fulfillment. Remember, when you get frustrated —

because it inevitably happens — you do have the power to make a difference, whether small, as in a single moment, or large, as in a transformative movement. All of it matters. All of it makes a difference. Your fulfillment and your work are needed by the world.

Section 1. Awareness: Turn on the Lights

In this section, you will learn about skills of observation, acceptance, forgiveness, working with chronic emotions, and, finally, practices. You will notice that some exercises focus more on thoughts, some on feelings, and some on actions. I call this the "access point" or how we get the material we need for our healing. We are, however, a whole system, and many times one access point produces effects in multiple areas of a person's Awareness.

We start the section with tools for observation. These tools help us, through observing the mind and the body, more clearly understand how we think and feel. This is a primary skill. A lot can be learned through observation. This book contains numerous exercises to help you develop observation skills. And it includes resources if you wish to continue this study further.

After we begin to see ourselves we can begin to change ourselves — so, after observation, we will move on to information and exercises to promote healing. In the Healing section, we will develop skills around understanding our history and how it affects us now. And then we will look at skills for healing our past by working on acceptance and forgiveness, so we can live more in the present.

Then, we will focus on the emotions and the body to work on chronic emotions such as depression, anxiety, and anger. We look at ways to work with — and begin to transform — these emotions. In this part, it is important that you use Awareness to see when and where you might be helped by an outside person. Whether that is treatment for depression, entering into therapy, or getting involved in a spiritual practice, it is deep work and it is important to know when outside support is needed.

At the end of the Awareness section, we will be looking at practices — the way we begin to move our healing into the world. I like to think of practices as mini experiments. The perimeters of the experiment help us see the results or our actions and thoughts more clearly. It is also an action that has therapeutic value, so it helps us transform both our interior life and exterior life. This sets the stage for the next part of the Life Fulfillment Formula, which is Connection.

Section 2. Connection: End the Root of Suffering

The second part of the Life Fulfillment Formula is Connection. In my opinion, the reason we are alive is to experience what life has to offer and, thereby, expand our consciousness. This expansion happens as we become more and more self-aware — not just inside ourselves but through connecting with the people and other parts of the world around us. It is our disconnection from life — our sense that the world is "out there" and we are "in here" — that creates significant suffering. So, in this section of the book, we cover skills for working on our closest relationships, like communication, working with difficult emotions, respect, and understanding others.

The Connection section starts with our inner circle of people and then grows from there. It moves from a discussion of our closest relationships to skills for working with our community, then our environment, and then our spiritual Connection. Each section provides several tools for developing our Connection as well as talking about why it is important to work in this area. Connection builds a bridge between Awareness and Purpose.

Section 3. Purpose: Make a Difference

In the Purpose section we deepen our understanding of what each one of us — like no one else — was born to do. We cover the fundamental steps of clarifying our Purpose and even create a plan for our work in the world. This plan can be used to help you know what kind of work will help you be most fulfilled. This section helps you move your work out into the world, thereby deepening your personal fulfillment.

Finally, I introduce basic concepts of leadership. This last section is designed to get you thinking and assessing where you might want to focus your next steps, as well as introduces the idea that living our Purpose *is* stepping into leadership.

These three areas come from my own experience and the rich experience of working with my clients. Clients who have learned the power of their own Awareness in changing the problems they face in their lives are ultimately living more fulfilled lives. You will hear more about them throughout the book. These stories should help you see ways you might be able to use the exercises in your own life.

Why Bother?: A Reminder for Ourselves

I have been asked the question, "Why should I or anyone else bother to work on fulfillment?" Some might say, it somehow got built into your DNA. Perhaps you are one of those people who don't know why you work in this direction; you just believe whole-heartedly that you should. Or, perhaps, you might need to be convinced. However, you may have started on this path and gotten overwhelmed, burnt out, or lost your way and started to wonder if fulfillment is really possible.

If you are still not sure, let's look at what happens when you do not try to live a fulfilling life. You suffer from painful relationship breakups that do not seem to make any sense. You live with anxiety and depression. Life can seem meaningless. It can be hard to make a living or feel satisfied with the living you make. Problems abound because you have no perspective — no lens that helps your problems make sense or makes them an opportunity instead of just a challenge. I think that is a good enough reason.

The world needs you to be awake, to be fulfilled, and to make a difference that only you can make.

AWARENESS: TURN ON THE LIGHTS

The most fundamental aggression to ourselves, the most fundamental
harm we can do to ourselves, is to remain ignorant by not having the
courage and the respect to look at ourselves honestly and gently."
— *Pema Chödrön*

All of our problems — all of them — can be lessened, changed or transformed by becoming more self-aware.

Do you know this? Do you use it to hurt yourself? Do you use it to grow and make a difference? We are all growing and learning — this never ends. We are all unfolding and becoming in each moment. Sometimes we might be afraid of, or resent, this process. We might even try to shut it down. And while that might work for a while, it does not work for long. Sometimes, we set out to make a difference to learn and grow, but we get overwhelmed, burnt out, or lost. In fact, this inevitably happens. You are not on the path unless you fall off the path at some point. It is important that we know that these are not failures — our off-roading experiences are gifts.

When I was 21, six months before I got pregnant, I got some bodywork done. There were two minutes where the practitioner held my head. She held it with such compassion. That was when I instantaneously decided that I needed to learn to do it. I went and studied bodywork, but that was just the beginning of my work with compassion. In fact, to this day, it is a central force in my work. However, I had days, weeks, months, and even years where compassion was hard to find. I could not find it for myself or others. I resented the people I worked with because I was giving energy I did not have — that I could not receive back. That was one of the times in my life where I needed to engage in Awareness work in order to be the person I aspired to be and live the life I was meant to live.

My life has certainly had its share of mistakes. Its share of moments where I failed to grow and, instead, tried to hide as a victim or justify my actions. What I have learned along the way is that the more willing I was to honestly and gently look at myself, the more riches I received, the more deeply meaningful my life became. Now, when I feel fear, when I face an obstacle, when I feel limited, I know there is potential that is right around the corner. This has created better relationships, more joyful work, and more peace inside my own skin.

Unfortunately, when we choose not to move forward — when we do not try to see our role in the problems of our life — life feels overwhelming. All of the challenges we face — that are a continual part of life, such as loss, suffering, and even death — overwhelm us and we fight more and more to feel safe in a way that it is impossible for us to feel safe. And then, we try even harder.

Wherever you are, keep in mind that being hard on yourself about what you do not know is never helpful. It is a process. Use the tools in this book to help you move forward rather than remind you of what you are not — or what you have not been — able to do.

It is when we begin to work on our own Awareness that we move from being pawns in a world of chaos to being active in the making and changing of our own lives. Awareness, and the concepts and practices around it, are relatively new to us. We can see its more popular beginning in the practices and theories of psychoanalysis. It hit popular culture in the 60s and 70s and has remained a part of our cultural Awareness since that time. However, Awareness has always been part of all religions — so it has been with us a really long time.

As I said before, the reason Awareness is such an important factor in fulfillment is that realizing what we think and feel and why we act makes a big difference in what we experience. In this book, you will learn about and implement the basics of Awareness. You can think of this as a foundation course in an incredibly expansive field. However, for those who have done some of this work, these tools never cease being important and effective. Each of them can be practiced wherever you are to gain insights and make positive change.

What is Awareness?

As I sit down to try and answer this question, I am noticing how easy it is to feel like I do not know. I think, from a broad view, Awareness is something we do not completely understand. People have thought about it for about as long as there have been human beings to think. Awareness, in my opinion, is having the ability to observe our own experience and make adjustments to our experiences that benefit our lives. In other words, if I am able to watch myself thinking, feeling, and acting — and, through this witnessing, I am able to make adjustments to my behavior that ultimately lead to my fulfillment — then that is being self-aware.

To boil it down, Awareness is about becoming the observer of our own life so we then have the power to create that life as we choose. Perhaps, ironically, the by-product of this is being more present. The less fabricated notions we have of ourselves — the less we are controlled from our own unconsciousness — the more we are we able to be with what truly is: ourselves, others, and the world.

What Stops Us from Being More Self-Aware?

Have you ever wondered this? There is no definitive answer. Some believe it is just where we are in our development — that it is a process, that we are *all* in different places in our evolution, and that has something to do with how self-aware we are. Some believe we are all self-aware at the time of birth and we are socially conditioned to shut down some of our faculties. Still another view, similar to that, is that the traumas of our life, large and small, contribute to our being less self-aware. I have come to believe — because of my own substantial changes in Awareness, because my work with others implies this, and since I cannot answer the questions of the universe any more than anyone else — that Awareness is a skill. A skill that we need to develop, though why we choose to develop it might remain, at times, elusive. However, once we choose to develop it we can become more skillful with our Awareness and therefore more fulfilled in our lives.

Within the following pages, I will offer basic tools for working on your Awareness. Practicing these basics can get you really far.

Steps to Developing Awareness

In this chapter we will explore a plan for developing our Awareness. First, we will look at ways to become a better observer of the mask and lower self and bring ourselves into stronger Connection with our higher self. Once we have developed our ability to observe or confront our notions of what is true, we can begin to use techniques that help us transform our limited selves/lower selves. Finally, we will use tools — which I call "practices" — to continue to develop our Awareness through living it in our everyday life. Practices are organized around nine value-based words: love, respect, compassion, joy, wisdom, truth, courage, humility and generosity. Each of these practices works with the mind, emotions/body, and spirit.

Here is an overview of the process:

Skill	Step	Part
Observe	Confront	Mask
Heal	Transform	Lower Self
Practice	Live	Core Self

A Basic Schema for Personal Growth

There are many tools that help us peer inside and understand what is happening. The explanation I am going to use comes from the long line of psychoanalysis and the offshoot I studied — Core Energetics. There are certainly other methods to help us understand our own experience; however, in this method, the person is broken down into three parts. One is the part we present to the world. This is called the mask, persona, or ego. One is the part that we try to conceal from the world. This is the lower self. The third part is the core self — also called the higher self or true self.

The reason I am starting with this schema is because it offers a simple, yet consistent, structure with which we can view ourselves and our behavior. It can be a bit tricky at first, but, since it is simple, it soon becomes an easy way to analyze our behavior.

When we are in the mask part of the self, it is almost like living one track of a multiple-track recording. In the mask, we think we need to be a certain way in order to be loved, accepted, and safe. We can get kind of caught up in this and even start to think that this is all there is of us. It is normal to be caught up in this in adolescence and early adulthood, but we often get caught in this part of ourselves for longer. When we get caught in this outer, more superficial, level, we lose our ability to observe — we lose our perspective. We become consumed with that mask self. We might start behaving as if we want to convince ourselves as badly as we want to convince others that what we are presenting is the truth of who we are. Sometimes, because of situations or social structures, we forget there is something more than this mask self. This can lead to feelings of emptiness, discontent, or falseness. This is why developing the ability to observe the self is so important and benefits us so greatly. When we realize that the mask is just a part of us — not all of us — our view of the world and ourselves changes profoundly.

Seeing the mask does not get rid of the mask. In fact, we never completely get rid of the mask. But, learning to see it is an excellent first step in developing our Awareness. Sometimes, just by seeing it, we want to put it away. It can make us uncomfortable. We feel out of integrity when we spot it. Sometimes, when people do not see the mask but are living from it, they feel out of integrity with themselves. They know that their outsides and their insides do no not match. This leads to a lot of discontent.

One of the most important things to do when working with the mask is to confront it — question its self-definition as our truth. Some of the things we can ask ourselves about our mask in order to help confront it are:

- What am I trying to protect?

- What is it I feel I need to convince people of?

- What is it I most want people to see and believe about me?

The reason we develop our masks is to cover our lower self. It is not that the lower self is a bad part of us — it is really the part of ourselves that is motivated by the classic "fight or flight" reflex. It is our survival mechanism. There is nothing bad about having a survival mechanism. We need it. However, the more we evolve, the more we see the limitations to this survival mechanism. It limits our ability to fully be ourselves, to grow, to get some of the best parts out of life. So, we acknowledge it and thank it for its role, but we do not let it rule the show.

The story goes like this: When we were young we likely encountered a number of situations where our natural reaction was to use our fight or flight instinct (the lower self). This was not accepted or might have even been forbidden by the people around us so we learned to act in a more socially acceptable way (the mask). So, in order to be closer to the truth about us, we need to reverse this process.

When we are trying to understand lower self we can ask these questions to better be able to observe what is going on. What am I afraid to have others know about me? What am I afraid to know about myself, about my motivations? The darker side of my motivations?

When working with the lower self, it is most important that we work to transform the fight-or-flight emotions. You can think of this like sludge at the bottom of a jar. One of the ways to get it out is to shake the jar so the sludge gets mixed up in the water. This way it is easier to dump out the contents and have a clean jar.

After a while of observing this mask and lower self, we get more in contact with our core self — our higher self, the truest part of whom we are. I often equate this with words such as "love" and "truth". This is the more expanded part of our selves. When we live from this place, we have the deepest sense of fulfillment. What we might learn through observing the mask and the lower self is that, the more we are able to be the observer, the more the observer is the higher self. That is why observation brings us to a deeper level of presence.

When Anna came into my office she was struggling at work, in her relationship, and her life in general. She was not sure which behaviors of hers were helpful and which were hurting her. Although she was a thoughtful person, there were many areas of her life where she was still not very self-aware. Toward the beginning of our sessions, I introduced the concept of the mask, lower self, and higher self. Like many people who first learn about this schema, it took a bit of time before it made sense. However, before long we had a shorthand for where an emotion or behavior might be based. Anna learned that she used her spirituality as a way to be detached from others as well as be disengaged from her own life. In this case her spirituality had more to do with her mask than her core. So, we needed to find out what lower self emotion it was covering. After some time it was possible to tell that one of the primary emotions was anger. Once Anna was able to see that her anger about having no control over her life was affecting her so deeply, she was able to gain quite a bit of understanding about how she had constructed her life and also do what was necessary to process her difficult emotions from the past. Doing so allowed her to easily change her behaviors so she could create a more satisfying life.

This very simple system can be very difficult to take in and understand, but, with attention and practice, it can be extremely useful. As you continue to read this book, I will reference this information so you can begin to see how these roles play out in your life. You can then use this Awareness to create deep and sustainable change, better relationships, and more fulfilled lives.

Observation

Our number-one tool for developing Awareness is the development of consciousness through observation. Observation allows us to see that things we think of as reality and fact are, in fact, perspective and perception.

The first part of developing Awareness — and perhaps the most important part of developing Awareness — is the skill of observation. As I mentioned before, observation is the ability to step outside of our mask and lower self and see them for what they are. There are two different ways to express the outcome. One is to say we get into contact with the higher self. The other is to say that the observer *is* the higher self. If you look at various practices around the world, you will see different ways of exposing the higher self. None of them are more correct or more wrong than the others. They are different ways for us to access and understand our experience. I think it is important to add that the skill of observation or the technique of observation is not new. It has not been created by me — possibly adapted by me, definitely explained by me — but these practices have been in place as long as people have been curious about their Awareness.

Observation of the Mind

There are different approaches to developing our observation skills. The one I am going to start with is the observation of the thoughts. During any given moment, we can have a multitude of thoughts going on in our head — some of them conscious, some of them unconscious. Meditation is a process by which we observe our thoughts. We allow our thoughts to float by. That is the tool I am going to start with.

Now, as I said in the beginning, nothing happens if we do not do anything. You can read this whole book, but, if you do not put it into practice, the change you see in your life will be minimal. So what I suggest you do to get the most out of this is create some sort of schedule for yourself. Even if you read this whole book from front to back without implementing any of it, as long as you come back and use each of these tools on a regular basis — according to whatever schedule you want — you will benefit from it. One example of a schedule might be spending five minutes a day reflecting on the content of this book. At the same time, remember: we all have our different paces and life requirements. Whatever you can do is perfect. Something is always better than nothing when it comes to your personal growth. Sometimes, even a drop is all we need.

Several observation exercises have the same beginning, which is as follows:

1. Find a comfortable place to sit or lie down — whatever way you feel most comfortable and well supported.

2. Close your eyes completely or bring them into soft focus. If you choose to bring them into soft focus, you will want your gaze to gently fall on a wall, ceiling, or other fixed spot.

3. Once you are comfortable, take a few deep breaths. Inhaling, you can imagine the breath gathering up tension in the body. Exhaling, you can imagine letting this tension out. Repeat this process at least three times and then let your breath return to a normal depth.

Exercise #1: Keep your attention on your breath. You might notice that thoughts begin to drift in. Perhaps there is a dialogue going on. Some of these thoughts might be mundane; some might be bizarre. Your job for now is to bring your attention back to your breath every time it slips away. You are practicing being the observer of your thoughts as they arrive and then practicing focusing your attention — for now, on your breath.

You might notice that you drift away for a while — that you had a thought and then started thinking other thoughts around it. You might get a little way down the road before recognizing this. That's OK. Simply acknowledge this process and the power that thought has, and bring your attention back to the breath. It is important to work toward openness rather than struggle in this process. Cultivating openness and acceptance is one of the additional benefits of this process, helping us develop our position as an observer. You can practice this as long as you wish. I recommend at least five minutes. If you can do it daily, that is fantastic.

This practice will help you develop your ability to see your thoughts so you become less identified with them.

Exercise #2: Start with the universal beginning given above. This time, instead of focusing on the breath, we will be focusing on the thoughts themselves. Observe what happens as your thoughts go by. Are you able to watch them like clouds floating by or does it seem like you are in the middle of them? Notice how involved or uninvolved you become. Do you lose track of where you are in the here and now? Can you see the beginnings, middles and endings of these thoughts? Notice the quality of your thoughts. Are they negative, positive? Are they about other people? Are they about you? Do they focus around specific events — perhaps events that were difficult for you in some way? Do they contain judgments?

Take a moment to remember this important truth — you are *not* your thoughts. After about five to ten minutes go by, take a deep breath and open your eyes. This exercise is more helpful toward the beginning of our work. Over time we want to decrease the number of thoughts we have so other tools become more useful. Initially, this is a great exercise to do for five to ten minutes each day for a week or two. Then it might be useful to do as a check-in.

The reason for doing practices like this — using these tools that have been around for so long — is that they help us see our thoughts and feelings rather than just being identified with them. They help us see the mask and help us be less identified with it. Seeing something is the first step in changing it. It is difficult to change what we are not aware of.

If you take a step back and look at your beliefs — what you are absolutely sure of — you are quite often observing the mask. Your mask often plays a role in conflict situations. Say you are angry at a friend for being late because you believe that being late is related to lack of respect. Therefore, when she is late, you assume she does not respect you. You get angry and want your friend to admit she is wrong. Your friend, on the other hand, believes that being respectful is about understanding that people are doing their best. As a result, your friend wants *you* to admit that you are wrong. As you can see, this is a conflict where the only solution is that someone must be wrong and must admit they are wrong. We have all been there but it does not need to be like this. Once we are more aware that we are acting from or identified with our mask then we can start to handle situations differently.

Exercise #3: The next technique requires you to think of a conflict in your life — present or past. Write it down. Then write down your beliefs about this situation as well as the judgments you have about others because of that belief. You can do this with any conflict situation that comes up. Eventually it might be possible to do in your head or without even thinking. This technique gives us insight into the mask layer of the self through the access point of the mind.

We can also work directly with our judgments of others. As we go through our daily lives, if we examine our thoughts we might find we are continually judging other people. They are too fat, they are too thin, they are too short, they are too tall, they are too smiley, they are too serious, they are too preoccupied. What we are basically saying is that there is something wrong with the way the other person is. These are our judgments. You can do this at a meeting, when you are walking down the street, or when you are at the supper table.

Become aware of the judgments you are using. You can write them down. A way to access them so you can write them down in the here and now is to ask yourself, "What don't I like about others? What makes me angry or frustrated? What do I look down on?" This is another way we get to see our mask in action.

Exercise #4: The final tool for seeing the mask through the activities of the mind is to recognize how we want others to perceive us. In any given moment, ask yourself, "What do I want people to see or know about me?" Usually this is something like: we want others to like and accept us or we want to be seen as powerful, in charge, courageous, certain, or confident. This is another exercise you can do in any situation.

When Michelle came to see me, she was totally preoccupied with what others thought about her. These thoughts stopped her from feeling authentic or acting that way. Even though it was clear that she was concerned about others' thoughts from the outside, she was not aware that there was a choice in the matter. She was wholly and completely identified with her thoughts. After spending some time observing her thoughts she was able to become less identified with her thoughts and, because of this, she was able to see that they were unnecessary and unhelpful. As a result, she was more comfortable with the partner she had chosen as well as who she was.

If you practice these things you will begin to get a really good grasp of your thoughts and beliefs as they are related to the more superficial parts of who you are — the mask. Observing the mask, as I said before, is the first step in becoming more self-aware.

Observing the Body

To observe the body, we can use the same skills and techniques we used to observe the mind. This can result in many different insights about how we relate to the world. However, right now, I would like to use the observation of the body to gain more understanding about your emotions, your self, and the lower self.

The body is where we hold our feelings. If you doubt this, think of a time you felt sad. How did you know you felt sad? You knew because you felt the cues in the body. Feeling is, quite literally, a feeling. Because many of us live in our heads, we get cut off from our feelings. If we want to be more self-aware, we need to be more aware of both our thoughts and our feelings. Observing our body can help us understand how our thoughts affect our body as well as bring us back into touch with what it is we are feeling.

In our bodies there are our immediate feelings and our stored feelings. Our immediate feelings might be what we feel after just getting some bad news. You might feel deflated, sad, or angry. Our stored feelings are our chronic emotions. If we are not able to process them out or come to terms with them in some way — transform them into something healthier — then they stay stuck. It is important to become aware of these chronic emotions because they are often patterns that repeat, just like our beliefs often control how we perceive the world.

To get in better touch with our emotions, we are going to repeat *Exercises #1* and *#2* above, but focus them toward the body. So, like before, find a comfortable place to sit or lie down — whatever way you feel most comfortable and well supported. Close your eyes completely or bring them into soft focus. If you choose soft focus, let your gaze gently fall on a wall, ceiling, or other fixed spot. Once you are comfortable, take a few deep breaths. Inhaling, imagine the breath gathering up tension in the body. Exhaling, imagine letting that tension out. Repeat this process at least three times and then let your breath return to a normal depth.

Exercise #5: Bring your Awareness into your body. Just realize what you're feeling there. It might be an itch or a bit of tension. It does not need to be labeled as an emotion, but it *can* be if that is what comes to you. Which parts of your body feel open? Which feel closed? Do parts of your body feel pain, pleasure, or tension? Check in with the physical sensations that are in your body. If you get distracted by your thoughts, return your attention to your body and feelings. If you find this difficult to do, bring your attention to your breath. Feel your breath fill your nasal cavity, your throat, your lungs and then the sensations as you exhale. Repeat this a few times and then bring your attention back to your body and noticing what you are feeling there. After at least five minutes, open your eyes and end the exercise. Like the other exercises, this one can be done often. Using it can be a great tool for developing Awareness.

Sometimes, this exercise can be difficult for people. It can leave them feeling uncomfortable. When I first started meditating, it felt like my body was uncomfortably twisted. At that point, connecting to my body was not pleasurable at all. So, if you feel discomfort when doing this exercise, just acknowledge it. Let it pass or stay as it wishes. See what else is going on in your body.

Exercise #6: This will be a body scan. Start with the universal observation exercise opening. Then bring your Awareness to the tips of your toes. Say to yourself, "My toes feel...." It might be an emotional feeling word like "angry", "happy", or "sad" or it might be a physical feeling word like "tired", "cramped", or "pain". Either type of word is totally fine. Take some time to move through all the areas of the body. For example, "My toes feel...", "My feet feel...", "My ankles feel...." Just say the first thing that comes up. Your answer does not need to be thought about for very long. If you find that most of the feeling words you come up with are abstract — like colors or all sensations with no emotion — this is a good thing to note. You might want to do another scan now or in the future where you ask yourself to come up with an emotional word. Going with our initial response gives us insight into how we translate the sensations of our body. Then, making sure that we find an emotional word for each part of the body gives us deeper insight into how we store emotions in parts of the body or associate emotions with part of the body.

When Jessy came into my office she stated that she did not feel anything. She felt completely empty on the inside. Because of this, she would inflict pain on herself to feel something. We used observation so she could connect to some of her feelings and emotions. At first, she was frustrated. She could not find any emotions. She did not know what to look for. I told her to report any and every sensation she had. Slowly, she began making connections between the sensations and the thoughts she had and actual emotions. Because of this, she was able to see how the events in her life were affecting her instead of needing to act it out unconsciously.

Exercise #7: Now, we are going to reverse this process. We are going to go through the basic emotions and see how we feel in our body related to each one. So, "When I feel sad, my body feels...." "When I feel angry, my body feels...." "When I feel afraid, my body feels...." "When I feel happy, my body feels...."

With these exercises, we start to get clear on what is going on in the body. Just like we can use the practices of the mind in any moment, we can use the practices of the body in any moment. If you take a minute three times a day to ask the question, "What is going on in my body right now?" it raises a lot of Awareness.

Our final two exercises use the observation of the body to get in touch with the lower self. We used the observation of the mind to get in touch with the mask. We can use the observation of the body to get in touch with the lower self. Not all emotion is lower-self emotion, but we can often extrapolate it to get a better understanding of what might be going on in the lower self.

Exercise #8, Lower self in a conflict situation: Think of a situation of conflict — either present or past. It can be the one you used before or it can be a different one. Think of what you said. Think about what you believed about the situation or the other person(s). Think about it as clearly as possible so it starts to feel real to you again. You might want to remember what it is you wanted others to believe. As you think about this situation, bring your attention into your body. See what is happening there. Is it tense? Is it relaxed? Is your jaw clenched? Are your fists clenched? Do you feel anxiety or a knot in your stomach? Check out what is going on. What is the last thing you would want someone to know about you in that situation? Or what are you most afraid might happen? Take these thoughts to the extreme. If you are afraid someone might win the argument, then ask yourself, "Why am I afraid of this? Am I afraid that my point of view would not exist anymore? Might this be seen as a type of death?" The deeper you can go, the closer you can get to the lower self. Perhaps you can see that you are being super-nice but the reason is that you do not want to let others know that you hate them — so you are overcompensating. Did you try to be generous and kind so people could not see that you were feeling selfish or that you needed them?

Exercise #9, Judgment: When you judge someone as worthy or unfit — too much of this or too little of that — what are you protecting yourself from? Think about a situation where you were in judgment of someone else. What were you feeling? It might not be clear at first. You might need to work at it, but if you feel emptiness in your chest or tension in your shoulders or eyes, just spend a moment with that feeling and see if you can bring out a statement. For example: "I hate you" or "I am afraid." This is the beginning of getting in touch with the lower self.

At this point, we have used the skill of observation to get in touch with our thoughts, judgments, and beliefs in the mind and our feelings via sensations in the body. We have connected our thoughts, beliefs, and judgments to the mask self and our negative "fight or flight" emotions to the lower self. We have done nothing to try and change who we are, but, as a result of observing, we may have also noticed some changes happening. We have learned that observation is a tool that can be used in a specific structure — like an exercise — and that we can use it at any moment of our lives. Observation has the greatest benefit when it is used frequently, but, no matter how often we use it, we get benefit.

Healing

Sometimes I have clients ask me, "When will I start feeling better? I have looked at all this stuff and become more aware of what is going on inside of me, but I am not yet really feeling any significant changes."

This is a hard phase to go through, but there is potential waiting on the other side of all of this. Usually, when we start feeling this, we are entering into the healing phase where we begin to see more of a return on our efforts. Sometimes, this happens suddenly — like a person suddenly knows they no longer need to act a certain way or no longer need to carry their story in the way they had up until then. Other times, it is more gradual and we start to notice that areas that once seemed challenging now seem less so.

Sarah, began working with me when she was very depressed. When she started, she did not realize that her deep fear of being alone was due to her mistreatment as a child. She knew she was not feeling well, but it took careful observation before she was able to sense the fear of loneliness under the depression, as well as the anger about how she had been treated. After she became more observant, she was able to see her patterns in action and begin to make some important changes. One of the changes was to write her father about how she felt about him. The result was first a feeling of relief, then loss, but finally her father came to her and apologized. This helped heal both of them.

Observation gives us the basic skills we need to make the most of — and to welcome in the process of healing. So, once we have become stronger observers of our experience, we can begin to transform it in ways that will allow us to be more fulfilled. These changes include transforming our story of the past and our negative beliefs and patterns, as well as learning the transformative skills of acceptance and forgiveness.

The Past: Our Story

Another important part in developing our Awareness is looking at how the past affects the present. Looking at the past creates the bridge between observation and healing. We look at the past — not so we can ruminate on it, but to learn how to be free from it. I think it is helpful to refer to the past as our story. The reason I like this is because it makes the past less fixed and definite and allows us to change it in ways that can be very helpful to our healing.

I am of the belief that the patterns we put in place earlier in our lives are patterns we repeat throughout much of the rest of our life. In other words, if we do not engage in this process to look at the past, we frequently find ourselves running into what we most fear. It may seem to us that we are powerless to avoid this. By looking at the patterns in our history, we can start to change our future. This process is most successfully undertaken with a trained mentor because the mentor's insights and ability to navigate the process will help you move forward more effectively. However, I will offer some exercises here. Any of this can be pursued in more extensive and very beneficial depth with a mentor.

The following will all be exercises you write down. Writing things down is as helpful to personal growth as is speaking out loud. If you want to increase your Awareness in any of these areas, then writing things down or speaking them out loud to another person can be very helpful. It allows us to see what is inside of us. When we do that we gain more Awareness.

Exercise #10: This is a narrative exercise. In this exercise, you tell a story about different times in your life — from before the age of seven, then between seven and twelve, then between twelve and nineteen, and then between nineteen and twenty-four. The story can be whatever pops into your mind from those ages, but one that is vivid and based in fact. Sometimes, because not everyone has memories from before they were seven, the story for that part of your life can be one that someone else has told you. Repeat the writing of a true story that easily comes to mind for each area of your life.

Once you write these pieces down, reduce them to their simplest elements. For example, the story is that a boy builds a sand castle, but the tide comes in and he figures out a way to divert the tide. This might be a version of a story, although it is likely that your stories will have substantially more depth. If you were to boil this down to its essence, it might be the use of ingenuity to overcome an obstacle. There isn't *one* right way to translate the story — translate it as it makes sense for you. You are looking to get at the essence of the story. Then repeat this process for each of the stories you have for each of the areas of your life.

Once you have these distilled stories, you might have some major themes. Take a few moments to ask, "Are these still themes that I see in my life today?" Usually they are, because they are basic themes we have all experienced, but they may play a more significant role in one person's life than another's.

Look at the significance of these stories for you. Is there something you learned in the past that you are using now — for better or for worse?

Exercise #11, Looking for patterns in conflict situations: Look at a situation in your life where there is a conflict or a problem. Where you are, or were, not able to act or be the way you want to be or are unable to untangle yourself from the problem at hand. Once again, you can use the skill of distilling. If you were to distill the essence of this conflict situation, what would it be? Or, if you were to ask a third party looking at the same situation, what would they think the essence of the conflict was? How might this third party characterize it? Once you are clear and have written down the essence of the situation, ask yourself, "When was the first time I experienced this?" Sometimes the first time is at a very young age. Sometimes it is later. Try to get as early a memory of it as possible because, usually, if you experienced it later in your life, you also experienced it earlier.

Here are some additional questions you can ask yourself about this situation:

- What did I learn from this situation that I still believe?

- What would be true or how would my life be different if I had believed something different?

You can repeat this process with any conflict or problem area in your life.

1. Boil it down to its essence.

2. Figure out when you came to believe about what you experienced.

3. Look at what you have come to believe and see if there is another view that is equally likely to be true and more beneficial to you.

Every time Tom got into a fight he walked out. Tom was raised in a family that was abusive and conflict for him had become so unsafe that he was instantaneously triggered as soon as there was a disagreement. At first he would just say, "This is who I am," but, over time, he began to see how his history was causing him to think that any disagreement was dangerous. After he saw this pattern, he was able to begin processing each situation so he could determine which ones were actually dangerous situations and which ones were ones that he might stick out.

Exercise #12, Personal fairy tale: This exercise comes from the expressive arts. This is writing the story of our life like a fairy tale. This exercise uses two different techniques that have been proven to help us with our Awareness. The first we spoke about before — writing things down. The second is the imagination.

This exercise starts out with: "Once upon a time, there was a boy" or "there was a girl...." And then you carry on from there. Try to write it using your stream of consciousness — writing down whatever comes to mind without censoring it. This is the imaginary story of our lives.

As you work through these exercises, you're going to see some of the personal themes of your life come forward. This allows us to decide whether or not we would like to carry them into the future. This is called "consciousness". Once again, if, as you do this, you start to become more and more curious about how your past is affecting your life, I suggest you find a mentor to work with who will be able to help you uncover these dynamics.

Acceptance and Forgiveness

To come to terms with the past, we not only need to become aware of it, but also to accept the truth of what it was and how it has affected us — and also forgive others and ourselves. Acceptance can be challenging, especially for people who have experienced traumatic events. People who have experienced trauma often minimize or reject its impact. Likewise, when someone has been hurt very badly, it is often very challenging to forgive the one who has hurt them. While acceptance and forgiveness are always helpful, they are not always appropriate. At certain parts of our healing process it is more important that we get in touch with and accept our own emotions rather than the behavior of another. And, it is important that we not only accept and forgive others, but also accept the consequences for what we have done and learn to forgive ourselves.

Perhaps we did not act the way we would have hoped we would, or thought we could have, when looking back at the situation.

Acceptance and forgiveness can be elusive. When do we know we have fully accepted or forgiven something? How do we do it? I like to think of acceptance as not arguing with myself anymore. There is no more inner debate about the truth or untruth of a particular experience. Sometimes acceptance even means I need to accept conflicting feelings. On the other hand, I feel I have achieved forgiveness when I can think of the situation and no longer have negative feelings about it.

Acceptance

Exercise #13: With these next several questions, you have the opportunity to become more aware of any areas of your life where it will benefit you to come to terms, as well as what you might be afraid of.

Ask yourself these questions:

- One thing I have a difficult time accepting about my life, but, deep down, know is true, is:

- Some of the things I feel I need to accept about my life that may be difficult to accept are:

- The reason I know these things are difficult to accept is:

- I will know that I have fully accepted these things about my life when:

- This stops me from accepting these things about my life:

- I would accept these things about my life if only:

- I am afraid that, if I accept these things about my life, then:

- What I need to do to accept these things about my life is:

Exercise #14, Speak your truth: One of the ways we can move into a deeper level of acceptance is to speak the truth about our life — making it more real. This increased sense of reality just naturally works to increase our acceptance of what was. For example, I have an event in my life where I have a fight with a close friend of mine. After this fight, I begin to slip into some story around it. For example, my friend was really unfair or my friend overreacted. You can see that these are judgments and, as I was mentioning before, judgments are about the mask. If, instead, I am able to state the data about what happened, this is the actual sensory information. In other words, "What I saw was...", "What I felt was...", "What I experienced was..." If I am able to break down the information as truthfully as possible, I will begin to see the situation for what it is.

Another way speaking our truth helps with acceptance can be seen in traditional talk therapy. When you see a therapist, it is customary to talk about what happened. Through speaking out loud about what has happened and having that acknowledged by another person, we are able to see the situation more clearly and come to a deeper sense of acceptance.

Exercise #15, Talk to someone who was there: This is why personal growth groups and therapy groups work really well. If someone has gone through a similar experience — or, as is the case sometimes with family members, the same experience — sharing that experience with someone who can understand what it is we went through helps us accept that experience. We come to know that this is what truly happened and these are the effects it had on me. As I was saying earlier in this book, when people go through a trauma, they often minimize the effects or don't recognize the effects. They do not see that what happened to them directly affects their life. For example, that their depression is related to the trauma or that their angry outbursts are related to the trauma. It is education which allows us to see all these experiences connect inside of us — how we live them out. This is another example of how we can use acceptance to help with our Awareness.

Forgiveness

Once we have reached a certain point in developing our Awareness, it is really important to begin to forgive. In every part of life, the faster we can forgive, the happier we are. If we ever start to think — like we often do when angry — that, by holding onto an injustice that is done to us, we are somehow getting the best of the situation, that is not correct. An almost-exception to this rule is when we hold onto an injustice in order to learn. For example, a woman who has been abused might benefit from holding onto anger long enough to get herself out of the situation. In this case, holding onto an injustice helps us learn to live in a different way. But, regardless of this, we feel better when we move into a healthy state of forgiveness.

> *Sandy was raped by her uncle. After years of excavating and processing her feelings she came to me to discuss her situation. It seemed that, despite her efforts, nothing was shifting. She felt stuck to this prior traumatic event. I asked her if she had truly accepted what had happened and the effects that it had on her life. She said that she believed that she had but still felt caught up in the negative emotions. I asked her if she had forgiven herself for what had happened and she began to cry. When I asked her why she was crying she responded that she did not know. I suggested to her that she might be still blaming herself for what had happened. When this became conscious — and because of all the prior work she had done — she was able to forgive herself for what she had previously blamed herself. Even though the situation was not her fault, because she had blamed herself she needed also to forgive herself. Letting go of blaming herself was a big step in her healing and allowed her to take actions that were healthier in her everyday life, such as expect a higher standard of relationship with others.*

Exercise #16, Humanness: Forgiveness can be a mysterious thing, especially around really big emotions, like when someone has hurt us in a very deep way. In order to forgive another person, part of what is helpful is seeing that person as a human being. Everybody, regardless of effort, is a work in progress and, knowingly or unknowingly, can hurt other people. Our forgiveness can come from recognizing that we are all on a path and that path is continual. We have not arrived; we are not perfect; and we all have to live with the effects of our mistakes. If we can begin to see that the person is doing the best they can — even if it does not appear that they are trying

— they are still doing the best they can. Regardless how it might appear to us in that moment, each person has to live with their mistakes. We cannot inflict pain on another person without it inflicting pain back on us. Even if it appears that the person is fine, there is a little bit of a deadening that is going on when a person hurts another person.

So, accepting humanness is part of helping with forgiveness.

Exercise #17, What is the price?: What is the price for me of not forgiving the other person? This is a more cognitive and rational tool. We go back up to the brain and reason with ourselves. What is the price of not forgiving this person? How does it affect my daily life? How does it affect my relationship with others? What is the result of my not forgiving this other person? The result can be profound when we are talking about being hurt by a parent or someone very close to us.

Exercise #18, Prayer: Another piece of forgiveness is intention or prayer. There is a point — well understood by those involved in Alcoholics Anonymous or personal growth — where we are unable to meet the emotional demands of life without additional support and to believe that we can do it without additional support actually starts to seem a bit crazy. By asking for help and guidance to let go of the hard feelings that we have — regardless of what we believe — we actually receive that help. You can attribute this to whatever you want — whatever your belief system is — but this is a good, solid tool to help forgive others.

Exercise #19, Forgive ourselves: It is also important to forgive ourselves in addition to others. We can use these same tools for forgiving others or ourselves. We can see *our* humanness; look at the price and how it affects *us* to hold onto these feelings about ourselves. Or use prayer.

Acceptance and forgiveness need to be continually practiced. As life goes on, we experience new hurts and need to find ways to come to terms with what has happened as well as let them go so we do not end up feeling heavy and discontented with life. If you find you are thinking negatively about some situation, look back through these exercises to see if there is one that might help you feel differently about the situation.

The biggest pieces of healing our lives are to:

1. Begin to look at where we came from.

2. Look at what is true for us and how it affects us now.

3. Come into a true relationship with that — the acceptance price — and truly accept it.

4. Let go.

These simple steps serve as a great outline; however, it is easy to run into challenges. For example, some people might have a really easy time understanding certain rules of how to heal the past, but this mental understanding might not translate into an understanding of their emotional experience or their actions in life. We could also have an inability to see how the past affects the present. Or, we could get glimpses of how it affects us now, but we are not able to fully accept it. Or, maybe we see a pattern but are not able to change it. There are so many different ways we can distort, misinterpret, or not see certain pieces of information. There are a multitude of therapeutic processes that can all help get us past those places in ourselves where we get stuck. When you get stuck the best thing to do is get help. It will save you a lot of unnecessary grief.

Chronic Emotions

Sometimes we just get stuck. We feel depression, anger, anxiety, or sadness. We are unable to leave these feelings behind. This might show up when we try to let go of the past. We might want to let go of the past, but feel unable to. We might want to be happier, but feel unable to. When we get stuck like this, it can be called a chronic emotion. It is difficult to work with chronic emotions on your own but, over time and with practice, it can become easier and easier.

Every therapeutic modality can help us get past these blocks. There is a benefit to the positive regard offered by Rogerian therapists; there is a benefit to somatic therapies, cognitive behavioral work, or goal-setting work. All of this work helps us with our Awareness. The key is to find what we need to help us move past where we are blocked. This is precisely what I try to do with my clients, and what I think we should all be trying. Find how they are stuck — because the basics are really basic. If we are not trying to understand psychological theory — if we are trying to be more self-aware and live our lives — well, the "rules" are not complex. It is all relatively easily learned stuff, but, when we get stuck (and we all get stuck, either due to a personal trauma or never having been taught the basics) we are usually able to gain the most ground with the help of a guide. They know the nuances; they have walked the walk. They can find where we are stuck and help us get past it.

The value in working with a particular therapist, spiritual teacher, or the like is not that they apply a particular technique so much as they apply a specific technique that is needed to unlock us in the places we are most stuck. So, if you are deciding to work with someone — or even reading books to work on your Awareness — what works can be different things at different times. There is a certain point where what was once most effective for us might begin to provide diminished returns. This is usually the time to switch the level we are working on, the modality, or use a different approach.

Practices

Once we begin to heal, we benefit from moving our healing out into our lives and creating a life that is healing inside and out. A Practice is when we use our recently developed skills and more healed selves on a consistent basis and often more directly in the world. We can see a lot of change and personal growth through a "Practice" because it stands like a mini experiment that allows us to see ourselves really clearly while making real-time change.

I developed the idea of Nine Practices to give people a way of doing their work as they go about their daily lives. I found that the more intentional I was with my time, energy, and attention the better my life got. While growing sometimes takes a lot of focus and effort, we are most effective in the long run if it becomes a regular part of our lives. The Nine Practices cover energies that:

- We work with on a day-to-day basis.

- Most people would agree have to do with our becoming the best, most fulfilled person we can be.

The Nine Practices cover respect, love, joy, truthfulness, humility, courage, generosity, wisdom, and compassion. In this chapter, I offer three exercises for each of these areas.

The Nine Practices were created to help us move in the world in integrity. What keeps us in integrity is knowing our personal values. We learn this by asking what is most important in a situation. Is it to be loving, compassionate, or respectful? When we know this, we feel more balanced, healthy and whole. I will be offering some of this work on values to you in the last section of the book. So, pay attention to which of these Practices feel really natural or powerful to you — these might be your core values.

Respect

From Aretha Franklin to your therapist or life coach, you will hear about Respect. While each person might have their own take on what is most worthy of Respect, really, everything is worthy of Respect. Respect means to honor all life. This means everything — people, birds, and even water. It can even be said that the fundamental problems we experience today could be shifted were we each to give a little more attention to Respect.

I think that, most often, when people think about Respect, they think about respecting others or being respected by others. Respect is something given, received, or taken away. Respect is seen as something earned by some or bestowed by others. However, I would like to talk about a *fundamental* level of Respect. On this fundamental level, others are respected for their life — their gifts — whether, in that moment, their gifts are challenging or enjoyable.

Exercise #20, Respect others: Think of someone you have a difficult time having Respect for. Maybe this person has a bad habit that has hurt you in the past. Maybe you have judgments about the way this person lives. This week, work to cultivate an attitude of Respect for this person. Maybe you can Respect the difficult path this person has walked in his or her life. Maybe you can Respect the life force — expressed in so many ways — that manifests through this person. Whatever it is, practice developing Respect with this person in your mind and heart.

Exercise #21, Respect yourself: In order to really Respect others, we need to learn how to be respectful of ourselves. To Respect ourselves, we need to have good self-care, work on our own personal growth, and learn how to communicate our feelings and needs. Frequently, people have an area or two in their life that demonstrates a lack of Respect for themselves. How do you disrespect yourself? Do you eat bad food, keep your living space in disarray, or cut yourself off from connections with others? Think of one area where you are not respecting yourself. For example, maybe you say yes when you mean no. Make a resolution to change this behavior for one week.

Exercise #22, Respect your environment: Respect for the environment is more crucial now than ever. It seems we have lost track of how interwoven things are and have come to believe that, if it happens outside of us, then it does not affect us. Our perspective around this is rapidly changing as we become more and more aware how our lack of Respect for our environment has resulted in a decreased standard of living for all life. This week I would like you to change one behavior that is linked to respecting the environment. Pick up trash. Set up a recycling program. Eat less meat. Maintain your behavior for the entire week — it wouldn't hurt to maintain it for your entire life! Let your action be a signifier of your Respect for your environment.

Love

When people talk about Love, they are frequently talking about romantic Love. People spend a lot of time looking for the partner who will Love them as they deeply want to be loved. However, very often, people forget that Love is a constant. And, while nothing can take the place of an intimate partnership, Love is a practice that does not require another person.

The basics of the practice of having Love in your life are receiving and giving. When we are fully receiving and giving, we are connected and in the flow of the universe. Here are some exercises to increase the flow of Love in your life.

Exercise #23, Breath : Spiritual disciplines around the world have emphasized the importance of a person's breath. The breath is a primary way we give and receive with the world around us. People stop breathing when they get tense or scared. Breathing encourages feeling and Connection to one's self. Every day for a full week, take five full breaths or more at one time. On the inhalation, breathe in Love; on the exhalation, breathe out Love. Really feel the fullness of your heart and the fullness of the Love around you streaming in and out of your body.

Exercise #24, Acts of kindness: Between "Pay it Forward" and bumper stickers, we are all pretty much aware of the impact small gestures of kindness have on the world around us. Many of us get caught up in our lives and forget to do the little things that mean so much. Shower the world with your Love. For each day this week, do something kind for the people with whom you come in contact. If you want to challenge yourself some more, do something kind for someone with whom you have a difficult relationship, or for someone you have been neglecting.

Exercise #25, See the Love: Does the world look dark? Do people seem not to care? Sometimes caring can all seem a bit Pollyanna. Small acts don't seem to put a dent in the suffering and despair we see all around us. But even in the worst of times and the worst of places there are glimmers of Love. No matter where you are, or the current state of your life, take a few minutes every day for the next week to notice the many faces of Love around you. They might be small — like a blade of grass through the pavement — but they are there.

Joy

Sometime in the mid-20th century, psychologists began to realize that what makes people happy or feel good about themselves is just as important as what caused their problems in the first place.

While mental health practitioners have still, for the most part, focused on dysfunction and its causes, many other practitioners in the personal growth field — ranging from spiritual leaders to life coaches — have emphasized the importance of what makes us deeply and profoundly happy.

Sometimes, people think that feeling Joy, or being happy, is easy and that it does not require work. This is not true. It can be just as challenging to increase our Joy as it can be to decrease our anxiety or depression. It actually takes diligence to open ourselves to more positive ways of being and to learn to see and accept the Joy and love that is a part of our lives. Below are five questions you can ask yourself in order to increase your positive feelings on a regular basis.

Exercise #26, When did it work?: If you find yourself in a sticky situation and it seems there is no way to make it into a good one, think about times in your life where you were successful. What did you do or not do that might be useful to this situation now?

Exercise #27, When were you happy?: Even if you are suffering from depression, this question can be helpful. Was there a moment in your life, however brief, when you were truly happy? What was it about that moment that made you feel this way? Don't be content with a surface view; look for little nuggets of Joy that created this great situation.

Exercise #28, What do you love?: This is a great place to start when you want to increase your Joy. Make a list of at least ten things you love to do. Make sure each day contains one of these joyous activities.

Exercise #29, *Why not do what makes you happy?*: If you have the tendency to create rules that keep you from feeling the Joy and pleasure in your life and you find yourself debating whether or not you "have time" or "really should," try asking yourself, "Why not?" If you don't have a really good answer for it, then go for it. Sometimes, you are only as happy as you let yourself be

Exercise #30, *What are your values?*: Time and time again it is proven that, if we live out of integrity with ourselves, we suffer. Make a list of what you deeply value about your behavior, relationships, and activities. See if there are ways you can bring yourself into a better relationship with your core values.

Truthfulness

From knights to sages, Truthfulness has been a trait that has been honored and respected throughout time. Truthfulness is to be honest and trustworthy. It is to be committed to speaking and acknowledging the truth, and to acting with integrity. When we have our truth we also have respect and love. Truth does not disregard the thoughts and feelings of others or ourselves. Nor does it preclude love, such as when one is brutally truthful. While, philosophically, there are many types of truth, the truth that is being spoken of here has a dynamic holism that is much more easily experienced than written about.

Here are three ways to practice Truthfulness in your life:

Exercise #31, *Know your truth:* In our quest for our own truth, how do we tell the difference between a more superficial sense of truth and a deeper sense of truth? Or, for that matter, with so many opinions and perspectives, how do we even know what our own truth is? In order to speak or live your truth, you must first know it. While all the world's spiritual and psychological practices have been concerned with this in one way or another — and it is really not a simple practice at all — a simplified approached can be formed around the practice of curiosity. Be inquisitive — like a child or a teenager. Ask questions. Do I really feel that way? Why do I feel that way? How did I come to feel or believe this? What is another way to feel or think? Looking at things from a new perspective helps us become more aware of what is true for us and the strengths and limitations of that truth.

Exercise #32, Speak your truth: Have you ever found yourself in the position of knowing what is true for you but holding it in? Perhaps, you were afraid of the consequences. Perhaps, you felt you just did not know how to say it in the right way. Speaking one's truth has radical consequences and, truthfully, these are not always positive. Throughout time, people have been killed for speaking their truth. However, while it is possible that this practice might ruffle a few feathers, it is also likely to greatly increase your sense of well-being and win you the respect and even friendship of so many great people. Learning how to speak your truth is challenging. An easy place to start is with yes and no. Usually there is some place in a person's life where they compromise themselves — they do not act in a way that is right for them for emotional reasons. Look for these times in your life and say yes when you mean yes and say no when you mean no.

Exercise #33, Live your truth: Many people talk about not feeling connected to their life. They feel as if they are not really living in a way that is right for them. This is an interesting part of our experience as people: we can feel separate even from our selves. In order to practice living your truth, you can ask yourself how happy you are with different aspects of your life — for example, your job, relationships, and personal time. Pick an area where you are not completely satisfied with what you find. Think of one thing you might do to bring this part of your life into better alignment with who you believe yourself to be. Practice this new approach until it becomes the natural way for you to think and act.

Truthfulness is not a destination; it is a practice we commit ourselves to. Through a sustained effort, we can create lives full of integrity that reflect our true selves and their unique insights and gifts.

Humility

Humility is knowing that, however great you or your accomplishments are, there is always more to know and something greater to be. It means accepting one's paradoxical position completely.

The practice of Humility is often misunderstood and, in my opinion, falsely applied. There is the concept of the ego as bad, and that Humility refers to the efforts to get rid of this bad ego. There is the idea that, no matter what injustices are done to a person, they should have the ability to turn the other cheek. And there is the belief that, to be proud of one's accomplishments, or to toot one's own horn, is conceited or arrogant. A risk that comes with the practice of Humility is the loss of a dynamic quality that affirms life through its sense of survival and creativity. However, that is not a reason to resist practicing Humility, as it remains important to our personal growth.

Exercise #34, The Humility to learn: In order to grow, we must recognize that there is more for us to learn. To learn, we must be willing to be taught. Being taught requires the willingness to question our own opinions when confronted with the opinions of a teacher. While Humility does not require us to blindly swallow anything we are told, it does require us to be willing to put our cherished beliefs on the line. Sometimes this is easy: for example, if we are practicing a new skill, like welding. We may need to put aside the idea that we know how to do it without help or that we see ourselves as handy. But, other times, it is more challenging, like when a teacher is questioning a fundamental way we look at the world. The practice here is to be willing to take in the message that is being communicated and to recognize that it might have validity and importance. It is best to be conscious about whom one is choosing for a teacher — whether it is for a moment or for longer.

Exercise #35, The Humility to be wrong: We are human and make many, many mistakes. This is the way of things. Sometimes our pride is on the line. We do not want to be the person who made "that" mistake. Depending on the size and impact of the mistake — and the size of our pride — we may really not want to be wrong. The practice here is to simply admit that we are, in fact, wrong. Perhaps that seems quite simple; however, the unwillingness to be wrong destroys relationships, communities, and our environment. To come to terms with our oversights, mistakes, and wrong-doings — and to admit these wrong-doings — is a huge piece of work that has far-reaching impact.

Exercise #36, The Humility to be right-sized: We are important and powerful; we are also quite insignificant in the larger scheme of the universe. Ironically, to act completely insignificant often has some of the same arrogance that thinking we are supremely important does. It acts like a mask. It says, "I know I am great, but I will act like I am humble." True Humility knows its strength, power, and insignificance and holds them without a need for attachment. To practice this, you can pay attention to when you feel too large or falsely small. Then, one needs to bring themselves into the truth of their own duality.

Courage

Whenever we are trying to grow or learn something new, it requires Courage. The unknown never guarantees an outcome. Courage means we are willing to move forward, make a choice, or stand out — not because there is a definite and desired outcome at the other end of our action, but because we know we are willing to face that unknown outcome. Whether it is good or bad — or whether it just *seems* good or bad — we, knowing our action is correct, will step into this unknown confident in our ability to handle the outcome.

Exercise #37, Move forward: Is there something you have been putting off because you are afraid of the outcome? Perhaps, it is making amends with someone, moving your business forward, or learning something new. Think about this step you have been avoiding. What might happen if you take it?

Go ahead and write down both the positive and negative things that might happen if you take this step. Now write down what will happen if you do not take this step at all. Sometimes recognizing that taking no action is actually more of a problem than action can give us the motivation to move forward.

Courage is to have the quality of mind and spirit to meet challenges despite fear.

Models for Courage are seen in the archetype of the warrior. Once set on a course, the warrior is willing to die if that is what is needed. While many of us do not face these real life-or-death situations, we definitely feel this warrior experience when we might succeed or fail at a new project, when we might be accepted or rejected by others, or when we step forward into our own growth knowing that the death we will experience will be the death of our beloved ego.

Exercise #38, Face your "death": Any movement or change in your life will result in the loss of something. Sometimes, we barely notice what we have lost. Sometimes, though, it truly seems like a death. Some of the greatest things in life can be like this — like committing to a relationship or having a child. The change results in us becoming a new person. It might just mean we are no longer identified with a problem that we have come to see as our actual self. It might mean we are entering into a new phase of life. Through articulating what might be lost when we take our next step — and coming to terms with that loss — we can connect to our Courage.

Think of some change you are bringing into your life at this time. What is something you know or fear you will lose as a result of this change? Give it a funeral. Acknowledge its importance and your feelings around letting it go.

Exercise #39, Who is your model?: One of the things I have found to be very helpful when it comes to Courage is to look for a model and to be inspired by that person's Courage. I get really inspired by the fierce Courage of Joan of Arc and the open-hearted Courage of Gandhi. Who are your role models? Hang a picture of them or a quote by them up in your home. Watch a movie or read a book about their life. Allow them to help you understand how to be more courageous.

Courage is directly related to our sense of empowerment. Courage requires a confidence in our ability to navigate a situation and deal with whatever might arise from that situation. We cannot truly step into our own empowerment without facing and dealing with the risk involved. Once we realize that the road is not secure — that there are no completely safe passages — and we set out anyway, making our best efforts to take care of ourselves and others, we have a confidence that is often called "empowerment".

Exercise #40, How will YOU handle it?: Think about a new situation in your life. Perhaps it is one you have not succeeded at in the past. Think about how you will handle it. What skills or resources can you use in this situation that would give it a more successful outcome? If you are not sure, ask a friend how they might handle it. Spend time before this situation imagining a successful outcome.

Generosity

When we think of Generosity, other words that come to mind are "volunteerism" and "philanthropy". Those are definitely two types of Generosity; however, Generosity takes many forms.

To be generous is to be giving — to give more than might be considered equal or "fair." Generosity stretches us beyond our limitations of character or situation and has us doing what is right regardless of whether the other person is doing what is right, too. Generosity is what helps us be genuinely patient with another person's anger or ignorance, or to be the person who does what no one wants to do.

Generosity is what makes the world a better place. It adds to the sum total of the goodness in the world. Generosity implies that something has been created that was not there before — that someone transformed their "no" into a "yes" just because they could. To practice Generosity is to practice positive change.

Exercise #41, Listen: Many people have the experience of going through their lives without ever feeling like someone took the time to really listen to them. Sometimes being generous means we stay silent and take a moment to find out what another person is experiencing and how we might really be able to give to them. This week, make space to really listen to the people around you. Put an emphasis on the people who are in your family or in your life on a regular basis.

Exercise #42, Give: Regardless of the current conditions of your life, find a way to give to others at least once per day this week. Examine how you feel when you give to others. Ask yourself these questions:

- What motivates you to give?

- Am I giving out of genuine kindness or are you hoping for something in return?

- How does my intention change the outcome or feeling of what I am doing?

- Am I able to let go of all attachments to the gift?

Exercise #43, Agree: It seems so important at times to secure our position. To be right and have the other person be wrong — to make sure the other person knows they are wrong. This exercise is an experiment in stepping completely outside of our ego. Try finding what is right, logical, sensible, and valid when you come into an interaction with someone who holds an opposing view. This view can be about you, about what to do, or even about a philosophical or political view. Try to do this in whatever area of your life you most resist doing it.

Wisdom

I am amazed sometimes by how we often choose to give up on our own Wisdom. How we hope that another person's Wisdom will deliver us from our need to know for ourselves and take the necessary action that is the result of that knowing. As a result, we deny others and ourselves the beauty of our own deep knowing. We become disempowered and, as a result, we disempower others.

Wisdom is the ability to recognize truthfulness, use expanded Awareness, and discern appropriate action. When we depart from our own Wisdom we can feel "less than" or even victimized. And we have been, in a way — we have victimized ourselves.

Wisdom is to our fulfillment what water is to our body. Quite simply, it is what makes everything work. From a spiritual or even humanistic perspective, we might wonder why we would ever shy away from something that is so obviously essential to us. Or, we might even believe that we don't ever shy away from it but, as we start to pay attention, we see the tendency is there. The smaller part of ourselves is often in opposition to our connecting with our deepest Wisdom. It might be helpful to hear that this Awareness is half the journey. Once we are aware of our own resistance to our Wisdom, we can make a firm and resolved commitment to being open to it from a higher part of ourselves and then we can use this Wisdom in our leadership and our life.

In order to be in touch with our own Wisdom, we need to spend time with ourselves and learn to hear the voice of our own truth. Without this Connection, we are incapable of being wise. Try this to deepen your own Wisdom.

Exercise #44: Spend 15 minutes in quiet contemplation each day for one week. The focus of your contemplation is: What is my truth in this moment? And what, if anything, could I do about it?

This apparently easy task is one that many people have a difficult time fitting into their lives. My suggestion is that you pick your time of day right now and, if you use a calendar or scheduler, put this time on the schedule.

Exercise #45: What might change if you truly connected with your deep inner Wisdom? Create a list of the ways you or parts of your life might change if you were to connect with your own Wisdom. Then ask yourself, are you willing to risk these changes at this time?

Exercise #46: Soak up some Wisdom. Who are you inspired by? Make a point to do some reading or attend a class given by someone whose Wisdom you think you might learn from. Do this sometime in the next month.

Compassion

What does it mean to be more compassionate? Why might we want this? To be compassionate is to open your heart to the suffering of others. It is to be a love offering to that which is in pain. Compassion, to me, is a healing action. When we offer Compassion to ourselves or others we are, in fact, healing ourselves or others.

I love Quan Yin. I have two statues of her in my office and two at home. To me, Quan Yin, goddess of Compassion, is a model for how I want to be on a daily and even momentary basis. Those who are not familiar with Quan Yin may be familiar with Mary — in my opinion, the Western version of Quan Yin. Pictures of Mary show her holding her child with a face of love. Sometimes Jesus is bleeding. Mary's face shows her unwavering offering of Compassion.

Exercise #47, Compassion for yourself: 9 times out of 10 people are harder on themselves than they are on anyone else in their life. For this week, pay attention to your self talk. Are you being judgmental and harsh with yourself? Offer yourself the gift of Compassion —you are doing the best you can.

Exercise #48: For this week, practice a daily prayer of Compassion. Sit somewhere quietly and think about all the people in your life that you have a difficult time with and offer them your Compassion.

One of the best ways to learn Compassion is through our own pain and suffering. Without a doubt, one thing we gain from hardship is an ability to be with others in theirs. Still, sometimes we might find ourselves feeling closed off or judgmental about others who are in a difficult spot.

Exercise #49: For this week, when you encounter someone who is having a hard time, take a deep breath, let go of the chatter in your mind, and practice thinking and feeling kind and supportive thoughts. Perhaps, it will be possible to remember a time when you were struggling and you can give the Compassion you wished you received.

As you have seen from this last section, small, consistent efforts can have a big impact on what we are aware of and, ultimately, on our fulfillment. You can create a practice around just about anything. If there is something you want to be better at, what is one thing that you can do on a regular basis to move in that direction? Do it and then take your next step.

How Awareness Can Become an Obstacle to Fulfillment

Shockingly, for some, the personal growth process can be used to block us from our fulfillment. I find this so frustrating, not because it happens — it is inevitable that whatever helps us will eventually hinder us in some way — but because some of the people who are willing to take advantage of this and do so for less than noble reasons.

One of the arguments against psychotherapy can be that it has people so preoccupied with looking at their problems that they forget about the parts of them that are healthy. They forget that we are all doing our best to live our lives. The argument has also been made that, in psychotherapy, people endlessly talk about their problems while only seeing moderate to insignificant changes in their lives. This is part of the Awareness trap, and I think there are portions of these arguments that are well founded. We can become fixated on problems or thinking about our life rather than living it.

The reason Awareness can get in our way is that we can become so involved in the process of personal growth that we are always becoming better — and then we are just involved in an endless process of navel-gazing. When we are doing this, the search for Awareness becomes a reason to be unhappy, dissatisfied, and to not take our next steps into our action into the world.

If you have engaged in personal growth work before, chances are you have experienced this at some time. If you haven't, chances are you will see it in yourself at some time. In fact, it most often shows up as we are beginning to be challenged by the action we want to take in the world. There are a million different ways to block ourselves from moving forward. In the end, if we want our Awareness to serve us, we have to be willing to get our hands dirty and move out into the world, regardless of what we know or do not know, and try to do our best.

The Purpose of the Life Fulfillment Formula is, of course, to encourage people to do their personal growth work so they can live happier, more fulfilled lives. But this is only one part of the formula. It is just as important that our lives are *lived* — that we develop our connections: to each other, to the earth, to spirit, and that we take powerful, life-changing action in the world.

While we need Awareness to make our connections and our actions as healthy as possible, it is not Awareness, in the end, that is our goal — it is to be in service of our real-life connections and actions. We do not stay in the place of observation to avoid moving into practice. We use observation to continually grow and change and we use practice to move that out into the world. To live what it is we have learned.

CONNECTION: END THE ROOT OF SUFFERING

"Everything that irritates us about others can lead us to an understanding of ourselves." — C.G. Jung

Personal growth — or the increase in our Awareness — does not happen inside of a bubble. Sometimes the first experience people have with Connection is inside of a therapeutic relationship after having a very long time of being unhappy or dissatisfied with their life. Developing this Connection and helping others develop it, as well — whether through relationships to other people, the world, or our relationship to spirit — is extremely important to our overall fulfillment. In other words, we can read books and work on ourselves but, until we can see change through the practice of what we learned, we feel that we haven't achieved enough.

This is not to say that working on Awareness is not important. It is *very* important. However, it is important in conjunction with our relationships to others and our actions in the world.

The second part of the Life Fulfillment Formula is Connection. When you begin to work on this, you will see really fabulous results, like more joy, less fighting, less stress, and faster transformation.

What is Connection?

If Awareness is being more observant and actively transformative in our relationship to self, then Connection is being more observant and actively transformative in our relationship to what is *not* us. We began to work with

Connection in the Practices part of the Awareness section and will continue to work with it throughout this portion of the book.

This section on Connection is based on the belief that we are not separate, but are, in fact, part of a greater whole. This whole is sometimes referred to as a "web". The idea of the web is an ancient reference that was taught by many indigenous groups; however, science has begun to confirm this as well. We are actually part of a greater whole, and what we do internally and externally influences this whole. Conversely, we are affected by it as well.

To really work with this and understand it, so it does not escape our ability to comprehend — which it can easily do — we can look directly at pieces of this interwoven experience. These pieces might include our relationships with the people in our life, with our environment, with our spiritual sense of things. In this book, any mention of Connection is based on the idea that we are all interwoven and connected; that everything is interconnected.

A piece of developing our Connection is looking at how we can cultivate our relationship with all people, places, and things. When we're talking specifically about relationships with people, our Connection is often called "intimacy". We will speak about the development of intimacy later in this section. While we often do not think of it this way, intimacy is also a good name for how we relate or do not relate to all things. An expression that is commonly used to talk about this general intimacy with all things is called "openness."

An additional part of understanding our Connection can be found in asking the question, "How do I understand myself to be linked to the big picture?" Understanding this gives our lives more meaning. In other words, what is our spiritual or philosophical view? How do we understand ourselves to be a part of the universe? This is especially important for us to challenge those parts of us that cling to duality or separateness.

As I said before, at a certain point it is very important that we begin to work on our Connection; otherwise, regardless of how much personal growth work we do — no matter how much we understand — we do not develop a greater sense of fulfillment. Similar to the Awareness section, it will not be possible to cover all of the nuances of developing our Connection, so we will cover some basics. Using these basics will go a long way in helping you get more connected on the different levels of your life.

Fulfilling Relationships

It sounds great, doesn't it? It took me a while to get this one, and some people do not ever know what this means. Because we have a past — and that past is never perfect — we can spend a lot of time in relationships where we relate from a less-than-adult part of ourselves. This happens in every relationship some of the time, but it happens more often when we have not worked on our relationship skills and our own Awareness. You might notice that, as you begin to make changes in your life as a result of reading this book, you will also see changes in your relationships.

Sometimes, unfortunately, change means some relationships will need to fall away, but the ones that do not — or the new ones — will likely get deeper and more fulfilling. For those who have not had the joy of being in a fulfilling relationship, I will spend a bit of time describing some of what you might look to foster in your relationships. Of course, you are the final judge of what truly makes you happy and fulfilled in a relationship, but these might offer some useful signposts.

- *Open communication:* knowing what you think and feel and being willing to share it.

- *Trust:* behaving in a way that is trustworthy, fostering trust, and being more trusting.

- *Respect:* understanding that the other person is an individual and should not be criticized for not being like you or any other person.

- *Love:* I like the expression, "Love is a verb." Healthy relationships seek to continually work to foster love through behavior.

- *Integrity:* the understanding that each person has his or her own path and it is not loving to take them off their path.

- *Partnership:* the desire to share life — its struggles and its joys.

Exercise #1: If you are in a relationship, you can use each of these relationship values to open up discussions. For now, I suggest you take a moment to write what each one means to you and how you do or don't see them in your relationship now — or in your relationships in the past.

The basic exercises outlined in this section will get you a long way in developing your Connection, especially with your partner or other people who are very close to you. As you practice these skills you will see your relationships shifting and changing. Sometimes, it might be helpful to get some outside support to help you make these changes as positive as possible. However, our connections do not just end there — they extend to everything we encounter in our lives. This will be the topic of the final part of this section.

What Stops Us From Being More Connected?

One of the most important parts of working with Connection in the Life Fulfillment Formula is to break down the duality that exists to some degree in most of us. In separateness thinking, there is a "you win" or "I win." In separateness thinking, we believe that, if we keep something for ourselves, we are somehow either helping or hurting others or helping or hurting ourselves — but never both. In connectedness thinking, we recognize that what we do to others or to ourselves has an effect on the other.

Most of us learned to think in terms of things being separate in our lives through our education by parents, teachers, and society. Some of us learned to see things only as separate because of trauma. You might have uncovered some of this in the Awareness section. We might learn that it is too painful to be connected or that Connection does not serve us. Or we might so believe in the duality of things that we insist on closeness but still do not feel a sense of Connection. Another thing that gets in the way of our Connection is a lack of skill. Many of us may not have experienced tools for interacting in a healthy way, so we see all sorts of problems in our relationships. And one of the reasons we start with Awareness is that even this can be an obstacle to being more connected.

Developing Connection

We have connections to our closest people, our partnerships, our family, and friends. We have a Connection to our community through our work, spirituality, and social projects or personal interests. We have a Connection to our environment. And, finally, we have a Connection to spirit.

Because Connection affects all areas of our lives, there are many different areas to pay attention to as we develop it.

One is to be aware of our power within our connections. At certain points in our development, it can feel as if the world is directing our feelings, thoughts and experience. It might feel as though we have little choice and that we are simply playing a role — either good or bad — that has been decided in advance. The truth is that we have a considerable amount of control over the way we experience and interact with others and when we understand this and what to do about it our relationships can become liberating rather than burdensome.

Another is to see our potential for positively affecting our relationships. Sometimes, the result of working with a therapist or teacher is that we begin to see ourselves in a better way. The more expanded or higher part of ourselves becomes evident in that relationship. You might say we are basking in the glow of this more positive relationship. This is a wonderful thing. Especially if we have never experienced a positive relationship like this before. This can also become unhealthy if we do not move this ability to create positive relationships out into the world. Just like with all other parts of personal development, we need to continually access the benefits of a certain approach. Therapists and teachers need to continually encourage their clients and students to grow and connect beyond the four walls of the office. We need to continually see our role and how it affects others — positively or negatively.

Essential Skills

Communication

A key piece to developing our connections — to other people, our community, environment, and spirituality — is communication. Communication, whether it is verbal or non-verbal, is one of the ways our connections can get broken, or, at the very least, where we perceive our connections get broken. For example, it is very easy for two people to believe they have a different opinion about something and so believe that their Connection is compromised. This is a bit of a myth. The difference of opinion does not actually create the separation; sometimes, it simply signifies a disagreement. However, more often than not, it just signifies a difference in opinion. Unfortunately, we have been trained to believe that this difference of opinion is dangerous to us and our values, when, in fact, different opinions are capable of existing simultaneously and do all the time.

A key to making communication work is curiosity. This is the desire to really understand what another person is saying versus the desire to have a "one truth" or "one way is right" mentality. We can get into touchy areas with this when we look at things like cruelty — for example, racism. This might be described as when another person's words represent destructive habits. This is also important to work with in a productive way. We will examine ethics more in the Empowered Action section of this book.

Exercise #1: Next time you find yourself in the situation where you are getting agitated or frustrated with the person in front of you, experiment with adopting an attitude of curiosity. Ask yourself, "What is this person really trying to say?" Or, "What does this person really want or need from this exchange?" You can practice this for as long as you like. I recommend that you consciously and intentionally use this exercise for at least one week.

One couple, Jackie and Sam, who attended my communication skills workshop, realized that it had been a long time since they had sat down and listened to each other. Because of this, they had begun to get angry at each other for the things they each did that the other did not understand. This slow-building anger was leaving them both feeling distant and angry. After just an hour of work, one of them remarked that talking for just a short while had made an incredible difference in how they felt about each other. While learning all of the communication skills can take some time, often we can see a shift just from remembering to listen to each other.

Using "I" Statements

One of the foundation principles of communication is the "I" statement. This means we own our own opinion by saying things like, "I think," "I believe," or "I know." The Purpose of an I statement is to speak what is true for us and to own that truth rather than assuming it is also the truth of others. The reason "I" statements are so important is that, when we speak and say "we" instead of "I", if another person does not feel the same way, he or she is likely to have a negative response. This person is likely to feel alienated and unseen. It also can create unhealthy power dynamics, which we will also discuss in the Empowered Action section of this book. For example, it can create an us-versus-them mentality. So, it is helpful if we learn to speak for ourselves.

When I am working with individuals, I sometimes use "we" to normalize behavior. For example, when I say, "We all feel angry at times." Or, "We all feel challenged at times to be the best we can be." The reason this is good communication is because it breaks down an imagined barrier; however, that is a subtlety that is best used when you have first practiced and understood the importance of "I" statements. "I" statements are very good ways to open up communication and begin to create stronger connections.

Exercise #2: Find a friend who is willing to do this exercise with you. Each of you will take turns speaking using "I" statements. Talk about your day, the previous week, your dreams, or your feelings. When you are done, ask your friend to tell you what he or she heard — also using "I" statements. Practice this until it becomes comfortable.

Using Information over Judgment

If we relate to others, it is only a matter of time before we have a conflict. As counterintuitive as it might feel, when we have conflicts is an ideal time to create Connection. One of the ways we can ensure this happens more is to stick with the information rather than promote blame through adding in our angry, subjective feelings.

So two main ways to distance ourselves from others is to 1) tell them how they feel, and 2) blame them for how we feel. These two really back down our Connection with other people. The responsibility we take in relationships that we discussed earlier is part of not blaming others. Another part is speaking the information about what has just happened.

Exercise #3: When you _____, I feel _____. I wish you would _____. It is a very simple formula. However, there are some nuances that are important to making it work well. First, only use data — information that is factual. What is not factual is when you say something such as, "When you give me that look, I feel like I have done something wrong." A person's response might be to negate what you just said because that is not what they feel — or are aware of feeling — on the inside. The more helpful expression is: "When you look at me with your hands on your hips and your mouth turned downward and your voice changes, I feel like I have done something wrong." The key is to provide the information that gives you the cues. If you provide the information accurately, it serves to make both you and the other person more conscious about what is going on. What you're saying becomes almost indisputable. It may need to be revised by you or the other person, but, one way or another; you will both better understand what the problems are and how to solve them. So, this is one way to be better able to work with conflicts so we can build better connections.

One of the first things I say to people when they talk about having a problem with another person is, "Have you talked to them about it?" Quite often, the answer is no. For some reason, people do not think of this as an important part of resolving a problem. I think this comes from a part of us that thinks relationships are just supposed to happen. This is not the case. In order for a problem to be resolved it is necessary for both parties to know about it. However, this is not all. It is also necessary for both parties to be able to speak about it in a way that is helpful.

Steve was one of these people. He was having lots of problems in his relationship that he kept bringing to his therapy sessions. He often had reasons why he could not bring them to his wife. She might react a negative way. It would cause him more grief. She would not understand. Through the course of our time together, I would model ways he could bring the information to her. He was surprised when he found out that she was actually more open to talking about things than he had thought. These conversations opened the door to a deeper and more fulfilling relationship between the two of them.

Say Positive Things

Our third tool for building Connection with others is remembering to say positive things. We can forget to do this for many reasons. However, when we remember, it is very powerful. For example, we might use the same formula stated above to say something like, "When you cook my favorite meal, I feel really grateful and loved by you." This may or may not be the time to make a request, though. A request may make you seem ungrateful or might set the stage for more of this behavior in the future.

But, regardless of whether we use the prior formula, giving positive feedback is helpful in creating more Connection. There was a study done that showed that happy relationships of all kinds have a three-to-one ratio — for every negative comment there are three positive comments. The reverse is seen in unhappy relationships — for every three negative statements there is only one positive. The moral of this story is that we can strengthen our relationships and make our relationships healthier with sincere positive feedback. The reason I bring up sincerity is that, if you fake this and just shower people with positive feedback, you might charm them — but the charming does not necessarily create Connection if the truth is that you are harboring negativity toward them. It is about sincerely reaching out to make a Connection with others.

Exercise #4: Try giving feedback to each person in your life at least once per day. You can try to do this for just one week so you can practice and pay attention to the differences that result from giving positive feedback.

Listening

Listening is perhaps the most important part of developing Connection. When we listen, we are, in essence, saying the other person or group has importance. Listening works when we show curiosity toward the other person and what they are saying. When we give ourselves time to listen, we give ourselves the time we need to really take in another person's perspective. One of the things that lead to breaks in Connection and/or conflict is when we do not take the time we need to take in what another person says. We hear a portion of what they say and we have already formulated our reaction. That reaction is then infused into all of our responses. We also do not take in the rest of what is being said because we are likely to throw out information that does not fit with our perception. When we do not take the time to listen, we do not give ourselves the opportunity to look at our own responsibility — why we are feeling the way we do.

Listening is one of the most important steps to making a Connection with others. When we do not listen to the other person, it actually does not matter if we do any of the other techniques. We have lost what is most important about communication — which is Connection. To practice this, we can stop ourselves from responding and move into a space of curiosity and listening. What is this person saying? What do they mean by it? What are they trying to say to me? What does it mean to them? Even better than asking these questions is just taking it in. Give the other person and yourself an opportunity to acknowledge this person's perspective.

Exercise #5: For one day or one week, practice just listening to what the people in your life have to say. Instead of adding something about your experience, simply see if you can capture the essence of their experience if you choose to speak.

Responsibility — A Seed of the Fulfilled Life

One of the things that cause us the most pain and discomfort in our lives is not seeing our own responsibility for what is happening. Maybe we blame other people — whether individuals or groups. Maybe we blame something even bigger, like the universe, by believing ourselves ill-fated or destined to have a negative outcome. A key to strengthening Connection in our life is taking responsibility and not placing it on others. This is not to say others don't also have responsibility in the ways they show up with us. There are times where others might hurt us with their words or actions. However, what we have control over is our own behavior — is changing the way *we* show up. We can take responsibility on each of the levels of relationship: interpersonally, with our community, with our environment, and even on the spiritual level.

While some people might not see responsibility as a skill, I think it is something we can become aware of and then practice — much to the benefit of our relationships. In the following section, there will be some exercises to help you take more responsibility in your relationships.

What is My Responsibility?

In just about any situation that presents a disagreement or conflict, there is an opportunity to practice responsibility. What this means is we look at what role we played in what happened. This does not mean we take responsibility for *everything* that happens — just that we own our part fully and completely. We have a voice, when in a disagreement, to either establish our rightness or look at what role we played. The first exercise is to think of a current situation where you have a disagreement or conflict and ask yourself, "What is my responsibility here?"

Exercise #6, The mask, lower self, and higher self in relationship to responsibility: Remember back to the beginning of this book when I introduced the concept of the mask, lower self, and higher self. It is helpful to ask yourself when you are looking at a conflict or situation, "What do I want the other person to believe?" (This is your mask.) Then ask, "What is my secret negativity that I do not want them to know? (This is your lower self.). Finally, ask, "What does the most enlightened part of me think is best in this situation?" (Higher Self) And, then this allows us to take responsibility for all parts of ourselves. We can use this tool to learn to take responsibility with ourselves for how we show up.

Exercise #7: When we get stuck and are unable to move forward in our communication or with a particular person or group in some way, we can ask ourselves, "What do I have to lose? Why am I unwilling to let go of my position?"

These next exercises are about beginning to take interpersonal responsibility. They can be used in taking responsibility with our relationships, our community, and our environment, and some additional approaches are helpful as well.

Exercise #8, Responsibility to be involved: It is important that we speak up and say what has value to us. When we do not speak up in relationships our relationships falter. A relationship needs each person to put themselves in. When we do not do this we are not taking responsibility in our relationships. It is the same in our communities. Without speaking up, your community does not have your voice. Without your voice and input, the community is less than whole and suffers from this. In addition, on the community level, we might have the responsibility to act ethically, or to not start problems between people. In an even bigger sense of responsibility, you might ask yourself, "How do I contribute to what I feel should not exist?" In other words, if you have a problem with injustice, ask yourself, "How do I contribute to injustice? How might I change my life to be more just and fair?" Or if you feel you are being mistreated, ask yourself, "What do I do to promote or accept this mistreatment of myself or others?"

Taking responsibility for our part in what happens can look different at different levels. For example, on the spiritual level, responsibility looks like showing up, asking questions, and being receptive. Regardless, it creates a lot of fulfillment and well-being when, instead of passing judgment on others' behaviors, we look at ourselves. Doing so, we are able to look at every situation that comes up and ask, "What is my role in this and what can I do to change it?" This one change creates a profound transformation.

Respect

Without respect a relationship is one of abuse and not of connectedness. In order to create Connection it is very important that we cultivate an attitude of respect. This means that, regardless of whether I agree with you or not, I respect your right to think and feel the way that you do.

Exercise #9: One of the blocks to Connection is making the other person wrong. Because many believe only one person can be right in a conflict, we often feel the need to make the other person wrong. Inevitably, this results in a lot of pain and resentment. To avoid this, ask the question, "What real harm will it do for the person to do things the way they want to?"

It is important that we learn to let people have the space to be themselves. After all, that is the reason we wanted to have them in our life to begin with. This ability to respect another person and let them be themselves is a foundational piece of creating Connection. We feel closer to each other when we know that *who we are* is respected.

This may create the question, "How can I be close to someone when I don't agree with what they're doing?" Ask yourself again, "Will there be real harm as a result of this person acting the way they want to act or being the person they want to be?" A simple remedy to this problem is to think about the other person and what they're all about. In other words, try to understand them rather than judge them. If you find yourself in a situation where the person you're with does things you are morally opposed to or you know harms others, I would return to questioning your own motives for continuing the relationship.

Exercise #10: How do you know that you are respecting yourself within a relationship? How do you know if another person is respecting you? If you are unclear, this is an important piece to do some work on with a therapist or teacher. A relationship cannot be whole if you are not in it.

Using "I" statements, remembering to say something positive, listening, and taking responsibility are four fundamental skills that help us develop Connection with other people in our lives. It can be really helpful if people get involved with some sort of group to develop these skills — ideally, a group used for personal growth purposes, because, if it is, there will be dialogue and attention given to the creation of Connection (or lack thereof). It is possible to work inside any group to develop your Connection, and it is very important to do this work inside your family. In this section of the Life Fulfillment Formula, I have created programs and groups designed to get people involved and working with each other on their personal growth.

Understanding and Healing

In addition to communication, we benefit from having skills to perceive who we are and who the other person is that we are relating to. Many of the skills that are used in the Awareness section to understand ourselves can also be used in the Connection section to understand others. We will be touching on a few of those in this next section including how our past affects our present and how to be able to better see the defenses and fears of ourselves and others in relationships. These skills help us look beneath the surface and understand more about what motivates a person to open up and connect or to detach. This section provides skills to help us heal and transform our relationships and ourselves in relationships.

In the Awareness section we talked about the mask, lower self, and higher self. This schema that we outlined in that section is also a great tool for understanding others. When we can look at another person and see where they are coming from, we can get a better sense of how to relate to them. When we, or the people we are relating to, are in the mask part of the self, there is a lot of judgment. We might feel insecure or closed off. As I said before, when we are in the mask, we think we need to be a certain way in order to be loved, accepted, and safe — whatever it is we fear. We can get kind of caught up in this. It is normal to be caught up in this in adolescence and early adulthood, but we often get caught there for longer. When we get caught in this outer, more superficial level, our relationships are strained, fake, and unsatisfying.

What often happens in relationships is that people meet for the first time; they put on their masks and try to be good enough to attain the love and affection they want. After a while of relating to each other and pushing all of the negative feelings into the lower self, the people in the relationship start to leak out these negative feelings toward each other — and the relationship takes a horrible turn for the worst.

Exercise #9: When we find this happening we can ask, "What am I trying to protect? What is it this other person might be trying to protect?" By asking this, we might be able to see more deeply into the other person's experience and come to a deeper and truer place of relating.

We often take for granted that people think, feel, or reason the way we do. As a result, we do not ask the questions we need to ask to really get to know them. This is especially common at the beginning of relationships, where we often focus more on being liked or accepted than on who it really is we are relating to. Before we know it, we are surprised by this person who we never really got to know. We are surprised they are acting in a different way than we would have. We may even feel betrayed and offended by their behavior when, in fact, the only person who has betrayed us is ourselves. In a way, we have betrayed the other person by not being willing to spend the time to really get to know them.

Exercise #10: Just like it is important to get to know ourselves, it is important to try and see others for who they are. Ask yourself these questions:

- What does this person I am talking to value most?

- How are they showing me their beliefs in their behavior?

- How is this person similar or different from myself? If you find yourself leaning in the direction of either different or similar, then try looking at it from the opposite perspective.

Everyone has hopes and fears — some that we know and some that remain hidden from us. When we are getting to know others, their personality can actually be a tool for understanding what they are most hoping for or most fearing. Some situations are clearer than others; however, as we pay attention to others we can gain insights into what they might be thinking below the surface. For example, does the person you are thinking of try to get along with others? Do they keep their distance? Do they speak their mind or withhold their feelings?

Exercise #11: Get a piece of paper and fold it in half. Write down what you think are five personality traits of someone you know on one half of the page. Then write what you think might be their motive for acting that way. Remember to stay connected to your compassion. It is not about being judgmental; it is about connecting with the other person — beginning to recognize their hopes and fears.

How Your Past Affects Your Present

As I mentioned before, our relationships are some of the most powerful ways to see ourselves. When we start building relationships, we can see our limitations or just our entrenched beliefs. The relationships we develop are a mirror of what we learned when we were younger. Our primary relationships taught us how to be in our present relationships. Sometimes, this works in our favor; sometimes, it does not. In this section, we will take a look at how our past might be affecting our current relationships.

Just like in the Awareness section, we will want to look at the primary stories or themes in our childhood or young adulthood. It is good to go back as early as you can. When you think about the stories, you will want to think about the themes and prominent emotions. These are often good clues to what is going on inside. You will also want to remember that, if there are no prominent emotions — or if there is just one — you should look a little under the surface to find what is really going on. It is practically impossible to go through life without having a few events that bring up strong emotion.

Exercise #12: Write the story of your relationship with your mother and your father. How did they meet? How did they relate to each other? How did they create or not create a life together? Pick out any themes you see in this relationship. Do you see these themes in your relationships? If you are younger, they may not be apparent yet, but, usually there are some similarities — or, if your parents' relationship was not a good one, you might have a very strong desire to do something different.

Exercise #13: Write the story of how both you and your mother and then father related to each other. Were you close or distant? Did you feel loved and cared for or hated and neglected? Very often, the way you related to each of your parents will show up in your relationships today — especially the romantic ones.

Julian wanted more than anything to have a relationship. Specifically he wanted to get married and have kids. However, despite his efforts he could not seem to meet the right woman. He blamed it on the fact that he was not suave enough and that he was not able to impress women. As we talked about this issue, it became clear to both of us that his limitation was not in his small talk but was a deeper issue. Julian was afraid to get close to anyone due to his loss of his mother when he was young. When a woman was interested in him he did not respond or sometimes even notice. For him, opening up meant the likelihood of a really big loss. While not everyone has a story like this, many of us are afraid to be close because of hurts in the past. For Julian, realizing what was at risk for him and making a conscious decision to face the risk of being hurt gave him the extra push he needed to get into a healthy and satisfying relationship.

While we cannot escape our past completely, we can continue to make better and more conscious choices in our relationships. If we do not do this work to figure out how our lives have been shaped, then we will likely have problems creating authentic closeness in our relationships. Our relationships will suffer from our unconscious tendencies to repeat the past. We find ourselves at challenging impasses where it seems we can do nothing but leave the relationship or spend our time wondering if we should. When we choose to do this work — hopefully with a partner, if we are in relationship — we can see radical shifts in the way we see the relationship and open the door to closeness.

Grief, Acceptance and Forgiveness

When we begin to work on this section of Connection, we deal often with issues of abandonment, neglect, or mistreatment — some of which might have been accessed by the previous parts of this section. It can seem as if the Awareness work we started is just the beginning. A new level of feelings can come to the surface as we move into deeper and deeper relationships. Sometimes we are not even able to create a relationship until we have done some of this deeper work.

There are four steps to this process:

1. Identify the problem areas.

2. Grieve for what you have lost.

3. Accept that what *has* happened cannot be changed.

4. Move into forgiveness.

Perhaps something came up when you were writing the stories about how you related to your parents. Perhaps you saw a broken relationship or unsatisfying relationships. Or maybe they seemed like good relationships but you noticed that there was a type of relating that was not allowed or an important topic that was not discussed. Maybe you felt controlled or manipulated by one of your parents. Or maybe a parent stopped being close to you once you hit puberty. It is not that these things become all of who you are, but if you can pull them out of your stories and find the emotions connected to them, you have started this process.

Exercise #14: What were the experiences you found when writing out your relationships? How did these experiences effect you? What was the cost? What did you lose?

Once you are in touch with what you might have lost in the process, ask yourself, "What might be a good way to facilitate my grief?" We have ceremonies when people die but, otherwise, we do not have good social systems in place to acknowledge and grieve for the painful situations in our lives. Sometimes, we erroneously think we should be able to move forward without doing so.

Exercise #15: Create a time to grieve. This likely will not happen in one day, but you can make it a point to spend some time telling your story and feeling your feelings. Maybe create something — like a drawing that represents your goodbye to that lost part of yourself.

When we give ourselves all the time we need to grieve, we gradually move ourselves into acceptance. Acceptance can be challenging, especially for people who have experienced traumatic events — "traumatic" in the general sense of any event that hurts us. As I wrote about in the first section, people who have experienced trauma often minimize or reject its impact. It can take time before we fully see the impact and are ready to accept it and move to forgiveness. Pay attention if you do not feel ready to do this work. When it is time, you will know.

Acceptance means we have fully and completely acknowledged the situation and felt our feelings around it. For example, I had a client who lost her father at an early age. Her mother, who was grieving herself, was unable to be emotionally present for the child. So she felt abandoned and confused by her emotions. This later manifested as her unwillingness to let anyone become close. Once she started to see that her inability to get close was, in part, linked to this experience, she was able to have empathy for that child she was and be gentler with herself. She was able to accept that this was a painful experience and understand fully what she had lost.

Exercise #16: What we need to accept is often what we least want to. The fact is we can't get back the years we have lost no matter how we lost them. What is it that you need to accept is gone forever? Once we realize that it is truly gone and that it is not possible to get it back, we have completed the acceptance stage and can move to forgiveness.

Sometimes forgiveness comes easily because we truly see the good intentions of the other person. But when it seems the other person has no interest in our welfare, it can be more difficult. Why would we choose to forgive those who have wronged us? I talked about this a bit in the Awareness section.

The problem with not forgiving is that the past then continues to hurt us and can stop us from building the healthy relationships that might eventually heal us and lead us to greater fulfillment. Whether we look at the primary relationships in our past — like our parents — or we look at other relationships in our lives that have affected us, we need some over-arching view that can help us put it in perspective.

Exercise #17: Who might you be if this event had not happened? What might you not have now if you had not experienced this difficult situation? Sometimes we find that the challenging situation helped us gain insight or challenged us to grow in some way that we might not otherwise have done. These insights help us see the silver lining, so to speak.

Exercise #18: What is the price for you of *not* forgiving the other person? How does it affect your relationships with others? What is the result of your not forgiving this other person? If you can see the damage to yourself, it can help you get unstuck and move into forgiveness.

This process is essential to the creation of deeper, more fulfilling relationships. So is this final piece — trusting ourselves again. One of the outcomes of these painful relationship situations is that we are unable to trust ourselves to make good choices. It is really important to find a way to forgive ourselves and learn to trust ourselves again — or, for some of us, for the first time ever. As we become more and more self-aware and more and more connected, we gain a sense of trust with ourselves that helps us feel comfortable opening up to others.

Practices for Connection

Giving and Receiving

Our ability to give and receive is one of the most important parts of developing Connection. Our practice of it helps us maintain these bonds. I think the best work in this area has been done within psychoanalysis and attachment theory. How our Connection is broken or established with our primary caregivers affects the way we perceive later relationships. Some of this you looked at in the last section. For example, we might believe we are always rejected by others or are never in the center or the most loved person in the group. We might also believe that people do not like what we have to give them. Or we don't want to receive from others. Or we withhold from others. These go back to what we first learned about Connection as we were growing up — about who we are in a relationship. We can see these being active any time more than one person gets together. Even if it is just the *idea* of more than one person getting together, we might see these patterns.

Exercise #22: If you start out understanding this, you can ask yourself questions such as:

- Am I more comfortable giving?

- Am I more comfortable receiving?

- What do I believe others think or feel about my giving or my receiving?

- What do I perceive about this?

These last two questions begin to move us into the judgments we have. Then we might ask ourselves, "What am I most afraid of with regards to giving and receiving?"

The exciting part about this is that, when we become more aware of the dynamics around giving and receiving, there is potential for changing them. Prior to seeing the dynamics — just like we learned in the Awareness section about becoming aware of our habits — they remain pretty much out of our control. Once we can see it, while it might be painful to see or accept about ourselves, it becomes something we can control.

The biggest problem with these issues around giving and receiving is that people start to believe this is their reality. In other words, they think this is how other people will always experience them. This is not true. We have quite a bit of power to change how others relate to us, starting with becoming aware. When we recognize this we see we can either choose to have a pattern continue or choose to find new ways of interacting where these patterns do *not* continue.

This area of work can be very deep and challenging, and it can be helpful for people to get support — ideally, from a therapist or within a personal growth group. This pain that keeps us separated from others can be intense and even overwhelming at times. Because of this, it can be challenging for us to get into contact with it.

What I was saying in the beginning of this Connection section is that our relationships are really a sign of our health and well-being. It is our connections with others — and feeling satisfied with those connections — that creates a sense of fulfillment in our life. This is a very important point.

I would like to refer back to Core Energetics at this point, because I think it is excellent for describing how these breakdowns with giving and receiving occur. Core Energetics separates people into character types based on the belief that common experiences produce similar patterns. Each character type has ways they are comfortable being in Connection and ways they are *not* comfortable being in Connection. In the Awareness section, we looked at mask, lower self, and higher self as ways of looking at what we want others to see and believe, what we most want to hide, and what the most developed part of us wants. This next part is similar because each type will have specific fears and pains and will want others to perceive him or her in a different way. It is this fear or pain that blocks people from Connection. You can look at the chart to gain some insight into this.

Type	Defense	Need
#1	Disconnect and Disassociation	Safety
#2	Neediness or Complete Denial of Neediness	Connection
#3	Compliance	Freedom to Do and Be
#4	Dominance	Surrender
#5	Perfection	Connection of Love and Sex/Acceptance

In addition to looking at the chart, see if any of these descriptions feel more like the way you connect with others. I think it will be helpful to remember that we all have these parts — that are hurt or broken off — inside ourselves. Knowing this allows us to have that compassion for ourselves and others that we spoke about in the Awareness section.

1. The first type in Core Energetics shies away from Connection on a nearly fundamental level. They might experience fear when other people try to connect with them. They might instead focus on impersonal connections. There is a sense of mistrust with the world. The feeling might be, "I am not wanted."

2. With the second type, the issue is around security of attachment. This type might not want others to know they care — or want attention. This type might also really *demand* that we have their attention, saying they're hungry for attention or that others are denying their hunger for attention. In a group, you might see this as

someone who monopolizes time. It might seem like they need a lot. Or the opposite — it might seem like the person is very self-sufficient.

3. The next type does not believe they can be their real self and still be loved and accepted. They get the idea that they need to put up a false front to maintain Connection. Often, this type will get resentful about how they feel they need to act.

4. The next type might feel they need to be in charge, or might be afraid of showing vulnerability. This type might feel more comfortable giving rather than receiving so that they can stay in control.

5. The final type tries to stop themselves from being hurt by being perfect. They might withhold themselves emotional or sexually to prevent this. They may come across as competitive because of their need to be perfect.

Exercise #23: Each of these types — for their different reasons — would not want to share parts of themselves. They would not be able to be vulnerable enough to receive from others. See if you can see either from this chart or in other ways what might block you from giving and receiving.

Exercise #24: The way we practice giving and receiving is by first doing the thing we have not done before — just like we spoke about in the Communication section. So, if we find ourselves going to the outside or not sharing our feelings, then we can attempt to reverse that. We can do this in some small way that seems as if it is a small and achievable change. With receiving, it might be as easy as saying, "Thank you" — acknowledging we have received something. Do something each day for the next week that brings you out of your comfort zone and helps you connect.

Love

Love is an important part of every relationship we have. It is important to tend to and to foster love in these relationships. While it is not common for people to say that it is important to practice love, I believe love is a verb. Just like running, we become stronger, better at it, and have more endurance when we practice love in action regularly.

As you know, love was one of the practices from the Awareness section. In this section I ask you to think about love not as something connected to another person, but that you have inside of you. I would like to repeat some of those thoughts here as well as add in practices where you can cultivate love between youself the people you are in relationship with every day.

Exercise #25: As I was saying, in order to maintain the love inside and outside of ourselves, we need to give it regular and careful attention. If you find yourself feeling frustrated or disconnected with someone close to you, see if you can take a moment to think of three to five positive traits — things you love about the person. You can do this with your partner or your friend or a parent. You can even take an extra step and tell the person one or more of the things that you really value about them.

Exercise #26: Sometimes we block the love coming from another person because of our own inability to feel worthy of love. If you find that you are disconnected or judgmental, check in with yourself to see if you really love yourself. If you are not sure, what is your self-care like? Are you eating, sleeping, attending to responsibilities, and having fun? If not, the problem might not be with the other person — it might actually be with you.

Exercise #27: Do you feel that a person or certain people should be there for you no matter what? No matter how you act, no matter how you treat them, no matter whether they show up for themselves or not? Sometimes we think that a person showing up in this way means that they truly love us. This is more the case in a parent-child relationship. However, in a peer relationship or partnership, expecting this is not about love — it is about dependency. Check yourself; see if you want someone to take care of you — whether it is emotionally, financially, or physically instead of creating true adult relationships and deeper love.

Trust

As you saw in the section on giving and receiving, we all have wounds that make it hard for us to open up. Because of this, it is very important that we are trustworthy in our relationships. It is also important that we demand this of the people closest to us.

Trustworthiness means that we do what we say we're going to do; we tell the truth about who we are and what we are capable of and we keep the lines of communication open to deal with inevitable misunderstandings. Trustworthiness is also about being willing to be accountable for our mistakes, expecting the best from those around us, and treating people with respect. It is a tall order and a very important part about creating and keeping Connection.

Exercise #28: Take a moment to look at the people that are in your inner circle. What would you say is your level of trust with these people? Can you count on them to be honest and open and to do their best? Can they count on you to do the same? Make a list of the people you are closest to. Is there anything that needs to shift in order to deepen the trust? If there is, how can you take action on it?

Exercise #29: How are you about your commitments? Do you frequently cancel? Or, do you find that you overcommit? Or perhaps you are not willing to make any commitment. Issues around commitment can show up anywhere — from going out to lunch to creating a long-term friendship or partnership. How are you about your commitments? Is there something you need to change?

Exercise #30: The first person we need to be able to trust getting into our relationships is ourselves. Without a deep trust of ourselves, we will continually look to other people to try and get security. Because of this we'll frequently wind up feeling betrayed. Make a list of three things you need to do to deepen your trust with yourself.

More on Connection — Intimacy and Partnership

When we're talking about Connection with other people we're often talking about intimacy. Intimacy is something we think will be the natural result of being with others, but is actually more of a practice that we need to cultivate. It is often practice that helps us overcome our obstacles to intimacy.

That might seem counterintuitive. Why would we block ourselves from experiencing intimacy — something most of us would claim to *want* to have in our lives? Just like other parts of Connection, though, intimacy is something we want in addition to being afraid of it. The fear may be conscious or unconscious; however, being close to another person means we might get hurt — and we are hardwired to avoid pain.

When people get into relationships — and, more specifically, when people get into relationships like partnerships and marriages — they often suspect they will naturally get closer to each other as the years go by. Then they find out after two or more years that, instead of getting closer, their relationship has plateaued. Some people falsely think this means their relationship was just not good enough in the first place and it is time to move on. However, oftentimes, intimacy can be improved if both people work to improve it. This is what we will work on in the upcoming exercises.

Exercise #31: What does intimacy mean to you? What helps you feel close to others in your life, especially in a primary relationship?

Negative Emotions

Anger and other negative feelings are often considered blocks to intimacy. However, what is more of a block is the absence of emotion or honesty about emotion. When people choose to suppress their feelings or are dishonest about what they are feeling, it is much more damaging than the clean expression of anger.

Many people, though, do not know what "clean" anger is so they choose repression over clean expression. Some people even choose to block all of their emotions and then expect their partnership will remain healthy because they are willing to do this. In order to have intimacy, we need to be fully present and able to share ourselves with those who we want to share ourselves.

I am not suggesting that people in a relationship dump their emotions all over their partner. Sometimes, in order to learn emotional regulation, a person must see a therapist or other helping professional. Sharing emotions, on the other hand, is when we are able to name our own experience and take ownership of it. Then we can talk about very difficult feelings without creating many of the problems we know from our pasts.

Exercise #32: What is it you are not sharing? Think about your closest relationships. What is it that you are keeping to yourself that might be blocking your intimacy? Notice if you start rationalizing your reasons for keeping this to yourself. If you think it might really create problems in your relationship then find someone you can confide in safely — like a professional — to figure out how you feel and what might be a good thing for you to do.

Our Greater Connection

Everything we encounter — people, places and things — are connected to us in some way. Sometimes, we lose this sense of Connection. This can lead to a sense of isolation, anxiety, and even depression. This perspective presents the unfortunate illusion that we are caught in a meaningless world where the things we run into have little or nothing to do with us. Our sense of meaning flies out the window and this can even leave us clinging to our close relationships in unhealthy ways to fulfill unconscious needs. In the following section we will discuss three additional aspects of Connection: Connection to community, Connection to the environment, and spiritual Connection.

Connection to Community

Our community is the group of people we feel connected or identified with, either right around us — like our neighborhood — or philosophically, such as equal rights communities. Being connected to community gives us a sense of meaning and belonging. Just like in our personal relationships, if we do not care for our Connection with our community then it can atrophy. But sometimes, also like in our close relationships, we can be unclear about what is the root of the problem. By looking at how you connect to your community you might be able to begin to ask questions that will help you build stronger and healthier relationships with your tribe.

Exercise #33, Connecting to your community: Do you have a sense of community? Many people do not. If you do, great. If you are happier with this community, even better. If you do not, who do you think your community is? If you have a problem with identifying your community, you might get some help from thinking about who you are, what you value, and what you like to do.

Exercise #34: Think about who you are in your community. Sometimes when we look at how we behave with others we can see patterns. These patterns are not bad in themselves, but sometimes we get stuck in a role that we think we have to play and we lose track of who we really are. What roles do you play in your community? Some roles that you might play are leader, follower, counselor, joker, or connector. The list can be pretty long but take a moment to think of a few situations with your community. How do you typically show up?

Exercise #35: How do you connect to your community? Write down ten ways you regularly connect to your community. If you feel you have a community, but do not often connect with it, ask yourself how you might be able to foster these relationships.

In groups, listening and speaking might look different but, just like with individuals, you should learn to moderate your behavior. If you speak a lot in groups or usually take a front-end role, then it might be a good idea to take a back-end role. If, on the other hand, you usually fade to the back, try speaking out more and taking more active leadership. In a group, pay attention to the overall group and adjust your behavior to balance both yourself and the group. One of the most common mistakes people make is they do not allow enough time for another person to step forward. Silence is a perfectly fine part of any group process.

One of the ways we can get stuck in community is by assuming that things are "just the way they are." In other words, what was true in the past is true now and will continue to be so. Sometimes, we have developed patterns of belief that perpetuate themselves with regard to others, such as, "No one cares about my opinion," or "If I give my opinion, no one listens." We might have developed judgments such as, "That other person is dominating the group with their opinion." One of the biggest culprits in breaking down our Connection in community is our negative beliefs about power.

One of the reasons I got involved with teaching leadership is because I was frustrated with what I saw. None of the models seemed to foster lasting Connection in community. On one hand, there was top-down leadership where the boss ordered, directed, or fired individuals. On the other hand, there was leadership — or not leadership — that, perhaps, had everyone feel good at first, but eventually left projects undone and people frustrated. Neither of these worked for me for, likely, obvious reasons. I wanted to create community where there was productivity, respect for the individual, and healthy expression of power.

Exercise #36, Negative beliefs about power: Sometimes it is helpful to first take a look at what unhealthy power looks like. Most of us know what it feels like to be in an unhealthy power situation. Write down your negative beliefs about power. See if you can find a more positive way to write these beliefs.

Healthy expressions of power are essential to Connection, especially when it comes to community. Most of us have experienced unhealthy power to such an extent that we are not even sure what healthy power is. One very important part of healthy power is that it is by choice. This means that, if there is a situation where one person is taking the lead and has more power than the other, the person with less power has consciously chosen to give some of their own power to the leader — by supporting the person leading — to get the job done.

Exercise #37: Pay attention when you are in a group, especially if you are trying to accomplish something. How do you choose to hold or not hold your power? Is this working for you? Why or why not?

Exercise #38: What do you think you need in order to feel comfortable trusting in a group? Check in with yourself — are you staying in your own power? If you feel you are, try acting this way to others and see what happens.

Trust gets developed in a group by individuals who are willing to stick their neck out so that others can begin to see that it is safe. Quite often, I do this for the groups I facilitate. As the facilitator of the group, I am often modeling empowered action. In these situations I take a risk so that I can both guide the response and help others know it is OK to trust. I build the container of trust as I invite people into it. I show them that they have a responsibility in maintaining this environment of trust and, when they do that, they are also creating an environment for themselves that is trustworthy.

Another key to creating Connection is creating a mutual-win situation. It was about thirty years ago that this concept made its way to the popular business literature. It was a relatively revolutionary concept because, prior to this, the common wisdom was a matter of having one up on another person — that one person wins and another loses — especially in business. You can still see this belief in relationships, communities, and businesses. You can also see its negative effects.

The importance of the mutual win is that it involves and requires a basic level of respect. This means that what is true for you is just as important as what is true for the other person — and not more important. It requires a certain amount of emotional maturity to actually be able to use this concept. We need to start by working with our own Awareness, develop skills around how we connect with others, and then continually amplify our Connection by creating positive, inclusive decisions for those involved.

One of the pieces of information we need to create a mutual win is both what is important to *us* and to *others*. Without knowing this, we are not able to meet our own needs and other people are not able to meet *their* needs. Creating this mutually beneficial option, and the decisions that we might need to make to bring it about, can be demonstrated by this simple scenario:

> I might to go out for Thai food. My friend wants to go out for American. What often happens is that people choose to compromise — which either means one of us doesn't get our way or both of us do not get our way. Perhaps one person says they will go out for Thai food or they will go with a third option neither wants. It is not that compromise is bad — it is just that there is a higher potential that can be attained if we understand the reasons for my choices — which might include that I like the atmosphere, it is closer to home, it is less expensive, or I would like lighter food — and the reasons for my friend's choice, which might be the same or different. Unless we look for it, we can't see what might meet both of our needs so we both feel happy with the decision. For example, what might meet both of our needs might be going somewhere close to where we are or going somewhere that meets our needs to celebrate an event — but we do not know that unless we ask the right questions.

We can apply a similar process in many areas of our life. It takes a bit of sophistication, but it is very possible. One thing that helps situations that require a decision that meets the needs of many people is to ask, "If this worked for everyone, what would it look like?" The great part about this is we can ask this question at any level — interpersonal, community, and spiritual.

Exercise #39: Make an effort this week to find a solution that works for both or all people involved. It might take a bit longer, but see how you feel afterwards.

The reason this type of situation — where we look for how to make it work for everyone — is so important is because it shows respect and a belief that the other person has value. When we demonstrate this respect over and over again by making decisions that incorporate others' viewpoints as well as our own in a way where everyone benefits, we gain a substantial amount of trust. This trust sets the stage for powerful internal and external change.

Exercise #40: Break down a desire or request into what is most important to each party involved. First, put the desire of person number 1 down, and then put the desire of person number 2 down, then 3 and so on. Ask, "Why is this important to this person? What is most important about this to this person? What is least important about this to this person?" Then, look for creative solutions.

A concept that is new to many people is the idea of leading with internal strength rather than external strength. When you are learning to dance, you learn that, to make a powerful turn, you need to use the inside muscle of your legs, not the outside part of your body. Most people turn with the outside and it throws them off balance. I like to call this leading with inner strength "leading with vulnerability". This means that you do not make yourself bigger in order to lead. You actually have the strength and Awareness to be able to show your faults and weaknesses — as well as your strengths — in any group you are leading. This takes a tremendous amount of strength. You have to know you can take care of yourself regardless of the response of the group you are working with. This helps create more respect and authenticity within the community or group.

Environmental

Our environment and its level of health directly affect *our* health. There is such a powerful link that I sometimes recommend clients clean out their house when they are going through — or trying to create — a major shift in their lives. It has surprisingly powerful effects. Of course, our environment is bigger than just our home. We are equally influenced by trash-laden streets, pollution, and climate changes. A little travel can show us that people and their environment are much linked. We can see how a culture or even a town grows as part of its environment. It provides deeper insight into the effects of poverty and war as well as landscape.

Exercise #41: What is most important when developing your Connection with your environment is that you pay attention to what is going on around you. Is there discord in your environment? Is your environment healthy? Is it suffering? What is going on? How can you listen better to what is communicated to you and then make positive changes?

Exercise #42: What does your personal environment say about you? Do you care for it? Is how you care for it a representation of how you take care of yourself?

Exercise #43: Are there certain environments for which you have an affinity, where you feel connected in some inexplicable way? Do you spend time in those environments? Why or why not?

Spiritual Connection

Spiritually, our development of communication looks similar to how we might develop communication to our environment — or to other people, for that matter. We might want to practice openness, curiosity, the willingness to show up, and listening to what is said to us. For some people, this is also a foreign concept — that we can develop an active Connection with whatever it is we think of as "the spiritual." Many people do this, however, and with great benefit to their life. Many of the practices associated with developing this type of Connection defy the written word, in my opinion, and are best transmitted from a teacher to a student. However, I do suggest you try the following ways of opening up this type of Connection in your life because it can have a profound effect on your overall fulfillment.

I know that this is a challenging subject for some people. There are a million views on a spectrum of Atheist to Fundamentalist. However, whatever your belief system, this Connection is, in my belief, available to you. It is best fostered by developing a sense of wonder and awe, no matter how you define your belief system. How can we not wonder and be awed by the vastness of the universe or the continual rising of the sun and changing of the seasons?

Exercise #44, Daily practice: Find something to do each day that connects you spiritually. This can be a walk in the park, meditation, or prayer.

> *Patti was plagued by continual anxiety. She felt the need to control everyone and everything. This strained her relationships and left her feeling less than satisfied with her life. Patti began meditating on a daily basis. First she meditated for 5 minutes per day and then 15. After a while, she decided that she would get some outside support and went to an ashram to do a meditation retreat. After the retreat she saw a significant shift in her life. Her anxiety had reduced. She had stopped a bad habit that had plagued her whole life. She upped her daily meditation to 45 minutes per day and maintained the positive results that she had attained.*

Exercise #45, Find a teacher or read some supportive books: If you want to develop this part of your life — and either have not started or have found that you got stuck — outside support might be helpful.

Relationships as a Personal Development Tool

Our connections can be a great source of both joy and pain. As we move forward with creating a richer, happier, and more fulfilling life, we will see our strengths, weaknesses and limiting beliefs show up in the faces around us. As we learn to be more savvy with our relationships and to pay attention to all of our connections, we become more deeply fulfilled. If you would like to know where you are in your life with regards to your personal development, look at the qualities of your relationships. They are the perfect mirror for the contents of your heart and mind.

Kate Siner PhD

PURPOSE: MAKE A DIFFERENCE

Knowing is not enough; we must apply. Willing is not enough;
we must do. — Johann Wolfgang von Goethe

As we become more aware, our influence on the world becomes clear. We are able to understand our own role in the creation of events. We are able to see more and more how our past influences our current perception. And, we begin to practice ways of being in the world that help us live more fulfilled lives. It is impossible to contain the results of Awareness inside ourselves completely — it will naturally find an outlet or expression in the world through our Purpose.

Inevitably, we all ask ourselves the question, "What is it I want to do with my life?" or, "Why am I here?" These questions bring us to our Purpose — a fundamental piece of our fulfillment. Our Purpose is the way we would like to make a difference in the world. How we would like to make the world a better place. When we are living out this Purpose we feel happier, healthier and more alive because our Purpose is a natural extension of who we are.

While some people might think that finding our Purpose is the end of the road, it is actually the beginning of a new journey. After we are familiar with our Purpose, we are soon faced with many challenges and decisions that allow us to continue to do our work on ourselves as we do our work in the world. This is a cycle that does not complete but continually brings more rewards and joy.

Why is Our Life's Purpose So Important?

Living our Purpose is the key to our fulfillment. Creating both an inner and outer positive impact through living our life Purpose will take us beyond what we might have seen as possible. When stepping into our Purpose this way, we will experience a depth of meaning and harmony. We become less afraid of outcome and more able to face difficult truths. We become this way because we are doing exactly what we are best able to do.

Each and every one of us will not feel satisfied or fulfilled in our lives until we understand the power we hold. For example, if I go to work and believe my actions and interactions are meaningless regardless of what my job is, this will have a negative effect on how I perceive my life and how much meaning it has. Or, if I perceive myself as a victim in all circumstances — feeling as though the world sets me up to knock me down — I will shy away from actions that might prove otherwise. As a result, I am likely to create situations that prove I am at the mercy of the world. This perspective will leave me blaming others, feeling resentful, and feeling stuck.

On the other hand, if I see my actions — regardless of my situation — as having the potential to have a positive impact and to be within my control, I will feel more positive about my life, more excited by my choices, and, ultimately, more deeply fulfilled and satisfied. More than that, if I see a situation that is dangerous, negative, or hurtful, I will feel it is possible for me to take action in a positive way. As a result, I will see even more positive effects and will likely find it easier to face even more challenging circumstances in a more positive way. This makes a profound difference in my life and the lives of others.

Think of this in terms of your life's Purpose. In order to move toward your life Purpose, you will need to feel as though what you are doing makes a difference — that you are capable of making a difference at least in your own life. Otherwise, there is no reason to bother.

(If You Have Any Doubts) You Can Do It

Whatever it is that you feel passionately about, you can do it! You were meant to do that thing more than anything else. Think about yourself in the terms that Alan Watts used: "You are the perfect expression of the universe exactly where you are in this moment." Or, as Ralph Waldo Emerson wrote: "The eye was placed where one ray should fall, that it might testify of that particular ray."

When you begin to see yourself as a being who is connected organically to the rest of the world — whose personal wants are whispers of the universe — then you can begin to see your work as imperative, but less personally driven. Of course, because you are doing exactly what you want to do, you benefit as well. Following what you love and exploring the ideas and options that emerge is a great way to hone your ability to envision a different future for yourself and others.

But what if you do not know what you want to do yet? No worries, the next round of exercises will help get you clear if you don't know and even clearer if you already have a sense. I think that our Purpose goes hand-in-hand with a vision.

Clarifying Your Vision

Vision

A vision is the difference you want to make in the world. No matter what it is — ending hunger and war, teaching parents how to raise children better, teaching partners how to love better, or however you want to make the world a better place — it is important to have a clear, desired end result. Your vision is your all-encompassing goal. You might never ultimately achieve this goal on your own — after all, ending world hunger is a pretty tall order — but your contribution will get the world closer to that goal.

Your first step is to create a Vision Statement. Most businesses use a vision statement to help them formulate their business plan, and it's a good way to help clarify your Purpose. Here's an exercise to help you write your Vision Statement:

Exercise #1, Your vision: Finish the following statements:

- What I want to change about the world is:

- One to three things that I think the world needs are:

- What I want to communicate to the world is:

- I want to help or serve:

- How I want to help or serve the world is:

- The kind of difference I want to make in the world is:

Now, write a statement of up to three sentences that encapsulates your vision — your Vision Statement. If you have more than one vision as a result of this exercise, pay attention to whether your multiple visions fit into one larger category. Remember, your vision can be BIG.

Here are some simple examples:

- To end hunger

- To live in a world that is free from violence

- To clothe the people of Vermont

- To teach the girls of rural Massachusetts that they are powerful.

Your Purpose

Your vision is something you may never fully achieve by yourself. It might not even be achieved in your lifetime. But, what role will you play in bringing your vision one step closer to reality? This role then becomes your Purpose — your unique part in creating this vision. The next step is determining what exactly you plan to do.

Many times a person can see more than one way they might work toward their vision. If this is the case, you might want to look at which is the most satisfying or most feasible.

If you are ready to move forward, here are some examples:

"My mission is to help people live happier and healthier lives through offering massage and acupuncture."

"Our Mission is to promote the value of learning, self-worth among students and staff, quality performance among students and staff, and transition for students to productive and responsible participation in society." — by Yvette Toro.

"Provide affordable, educational, and outdoor recreational activities in a safe, clean, and inviting environment for people of all ages through sound business and management practices."

Exercise #2, Your mission: Complete these statements:

- I am good at:

- I love to:

- I am interested in:

- I have had prior success when:

- I see myself personally contributing to my vision by:

It is so much easier to get where you are going when you know where you are going.

Claudia, a woman who attended my Make it Happen program, felt she was not reaching her goals. She had really great ideas but they never seemed to manifest the way she wanted them to. She felt scattered — like she had too many ideas. As we did the work on her vision, she realized the unifying element behind what seemed to be scattered work. This helped her feel more focused. When we got to the level of the mission, she again felt stuck. Which one of her ideas was she going to take action on? After I pointed out that this was not a final answer but rather a starting place and gave her criteria to figure out what she wanted to do based on what she wanted in her life, she was able to make a choice about her direction and finally see the results she wanted to see.

Just a Little More Clarity

If your Purpose is a bit vague, perhaps it says more about how you are going to do things but doesn't specifically say what. Boil it down just a bit more. Write exactly what you are going to do. Try to imagine answering the question, "What do you do?" as clearly as possible. For some people this is too big of a leap; they cannot see what they would do with their unique combination of skills. Do not stay here long without getting help. This can be a critical make-or-break juncture. Help will move you right past it.

Where to Start: Values and Goals

Once you are clear on your Purpose and vision, you need to create a plan to achieve them. To start, you need two pieces — "values" and "goals."

Goals are the end results you are trying to achieve. They are the "what" in your plan. Values are the "how" of the plan. To understand the difference, here's an example. Business ventures are designed to make money. A goal might be to achieve a certain level of sales or amount of money, similar to any other business designed to make money. However, any two businesses might have drastically different values. One might value respect and sustainability. The other might value speed of return on investments. The way each business reaches its goals is influenced by individual and company values.

Values

Values allow us to not only make decisions and move forward but to move forward in a way that feels right to us and creates the type of impact we want to create. We can use values in any area of our life to get clear about our best choice or make sure that we are going to "feel good" while we are reaching our goals.

Here are a couple of examples of values from my organizations:

Example 1: Non-profit developed to stop gender-based violence.

- Empowerment: We seek to empower all people at every level of the organization and its programs.

- Awareness: Our organization's goal is to educate others about the nuances of women's leadership and gender-based violence.

- Effectiveness: Our programs and methods are successful at empowering women and decreasing gender-based violence.

- Sustainability: Our program and its systems are designed to be balanced and harmonious.

Example 2: Therapy Group.

- Client-centered: We listen to each client's individual needs and provide for those needs.

- Holistic: We effectively treat each client's symptoms while never losing sight of the whole person.

- Grounded: We choose quality and knowledgeable practitioners of effective disciplines.

- Balanced: We carefully balance the art and science of healing.

- Available: We offer extended hours and multiple practitioners for client convenience.

- Effective: We craft treatment programs that pay attention to the most relevant treatment, including complementary and supportive alternatives.

- Compassionate: We maintain strong, supportive relationships with our clients.

Exercise #3, Value sheet: Make a list of values you will use while acting and interacting. Then, write a short phrase that describes these values. If you are not sure, think of some values that are important to you in everyday life. Also, here is a short list of some common values:

Abundance	Devotion	Leadership
Acceptance	Economy	Open-mindedness
Adaptability	Efficiency	Originality
Altruism	Empathy	Philanthropy
Awareness	Enjoyment	Pragmatism
Balance	Expertise	Recognition
Bravery	Expressiveness	Refinement
Charity	Fairness	Skillfulness
Clarity	Flexibility	Spirituality
Congruency	Giving	Synergy
Consistency	Honesty	Thoroughness
Cooperation	Intelligence	Vision
Creativity	Joy	Wisdom
Decisiveness	Knowledge	

Write your list of five to ten values and put a star next to your top three values. You can use your values to guide your decision-making process at any point. If you are unsure as to what to do, you can refer back to your values to see what you aspire to be. Without values, it is challenging to figure out what is best to do.

People often worry that, if they try to live their Purpose in the world, then they will need to sacrifice their values. However, values help people make decisions and have the type of impact they want to have. The following is an example:

Jack was building his business and, for him, marketing seemed to be a bit sleazy. So, I asked him what marketing might look like if he did it in alignment with his values. He was able to quickly see what might work for him and get his business off to a strong start.

Goals

Long-Term Goals

A clear goal requires the ability to step outside the current circumstances and look at the larger picture. In order to set appropriate objectives, make sure you are aware of your Purpose and vision before you set your goals. Having the wrong goal, or even having goals that are slightly off the mark, will make the work of getting what you want to get accomplished much harder — meaning it will take that much more time. Perhaps your goal is to feed 100 people a month or decrease the number of women on welfare by providing jobs with decent wages. Some of your goals might be a bit more personally oriented, like how much money you want to make or how much time you want to work, but you have to make sure they are clear, measurable, and that they outline the specifics of your mission.

Exercise #4, Goal sheet: If you achieve your objectives, with your vision, what will you have accomplished? These are your big goals. List three to ten long-term goals.

Exercise #5, Where to get started: At this point in time, you have a vision, a mission, and a list of goals. When you look at your list of goals, ask yourself if any of your goals need to be accomplished before others or are more important than others. Some of the ways to decide this are to ask yourself:

- Does this need to get done in order for me to accomplish other goals?

- Is this likely to have the strongest positive effect if I do it?

- Is this likely to have a strong negative effect if I do not do it?

- Is this essential to my end goal and must it always be a focus?

Put your goals in their order of importance. Don't worry about being exact with this. It is just basic organization of your ideas so that really important things do not get lost and not-so-important things do not get all your attention:

The previous exercises provide you with the skeleton of your plan. Using these, you will be able to build the structure that holds your dream together. Don't be concerned that you have forgotten an important aspect or lack an important piece of the puzzle. You can return to these exercises at any time to clarify or adjust your plan.

Exercise #6, Working backwards: Write a goal down on the right-hand side of a page. To the left of it, write what you need in order to make that goal happen. To the right of that, write what you need in order to have that happen. Keep doing this exercise until you find that you have what you need. Do this with each of your goals.

Short-Term Goals and Action Steps

To bring your plan closer to reality, you will need to establish short-term goals. When creating your short-term goals, make them specific, measurable, action oriented and timely.

Exercise #7, Working forward: Take your work from Exercise #6. Start on the left-hand side this time. Ask yourself, "What do I need to do to get myself to the next step?" Repeat this question until you have explored all the options or have found a step that you are satisfied with. Then, define this goal. What exactly do you need to do? Call someone? Take a class? Do research? How will you know that you have done it? What will you have by the time you are done — information, permissions, another question? Is it something that you can do?

You will not move your plan forward if your goals are to wait for other people to do things. When are you to accomplish this — tomorrow, next week, next month?

Repeat this exercise with all of your goals.

Exercise #8, Action steps: What can you do now? Look at the work you have done on your short-term goals. What on the list can you start working on right away? Take these actions and put them into a planner. What will you work on today, tomorrow, or for the rest of the week?

Exercise #9, Weekly re-assessment: Assess your short-term goals and actions weekly, if not daily. In order to keep yourself on track, you must continue to look at your plan and figure out what action steps can be taken as well as revise any areas that have changed due to new information.

Here is what a program participant has to say:

Before I started working with Kate, I had visions and ideas but felt overwhelmed by the magnitude of them. I was convinced I did not have the tools, energy, skills, charisma to manifest these visions. The three most significant things that I learned from the WLC program and Kate are. 1.) The only thing standing between me and my visions is my fear. 2.) All my excuses are just old tapes and I have the ability to change them. 3.) I have a much better understanding of how groups work, how to keep a group together, functional, and worthy of everyone's time.

Heart-Centered Strategy/Remember Your Values

It is not enough just to be able to plan. In order to bring something truly purposeful into being, you will also need to pay attention each step of the way to whether you are adhering to your values. It is important that every action step you take, every person with whom you interact, and every goal you reach upholds the values to which you are committed.

Exercise #10, In this moment: Go back to Exercise #3 — your Value Sheet. Write a statement about what you can do right now to make each value a part of what you are doing. Hang these statements in a place you will frequently see them.

Exercise #11, Negative beliefs: Sometimes we have really good intentions, but when it comes right down to it, we don't really believe that that is the way the world works. These negative beliefs prevent us from seeing opportunities and also stop us from truly acting from our values. Take a moment to write out all of your doubts, fears, and negative predictions about how the world works on one half of a sheet of paper. Then, rephrase each belief to something more positive yet still fully believable.

Exercise #12: Review the "why" of your project. Write down and continue to revisit why you are doing the project you are doing.

These exercises will help you get together a basic plan that will help you with many aspects of living your life's Purpose. It can help you get more focused at your job, create a feeling of Purpose in your life, or create a new project or business. Many people do not take the time to drill down to the essence of what they are doing and, because of this, there is a loss of meaning and, therefore, fulfillment.

Bringing Your Purpose into the World

When trying to get clear on our Purpose or trying to take that Purpose out into the world we eventually get stuck. Once people make a decision to do something or get clear on something like their Purpose, the next thing that happens is they get stuck. Fear replaces the enthusiasm they felt just days or moments before.

There are three sizable culprits (habits) that can stop us in our tracks. They result in a loss of drive, focus, enthusiasm, and happiness. Chances are, if you are losing steam, there are some habits causing this that could benefit from being remedied. For example:

Perfectionism: A perfectionist sometimes gives up before even starting. Their standards are so high that starting new tasks is difficult because there is no way to master something and begin it at the same time.

Exercise #13: Intentionally fail or move forward before you are ready. Might sound crazy, but it can be highly effective. Figure out what you are most afraid of having happen and then bring it on yourself. Once you live through a couple of your fears you will be less invested in being perfect.

Shoulds: Some people have come to believe there are absolutes guiding their life. For example: a person believes he or she should be an accountant instead of an artist. Or that other people should have done something different. Or he or she should have known better.

Exercise #14: We do not get very far when our baseline belief is that we are supposed to think, feel and act a different way than we do. So, spend a week reminding yourself that everything that you think, feel and do is just perfect for who you are. If you have a hard time doing it for yourself, try doing it for someone else that you can see is telling themselves what they should do and be all the time.

Same Wrong Way: People often think their success depends on their ability to do it the way others have done it even if they are completely unlike the others they are comparing themselves to. So they compare themselves to others, looking for what is lacking. Eventually, if you look hard enough, you can find it.

Exercise #15: Find 10 out-of-the-norm examples. If you think you need to be rich to get rich look for people who triumphed over poverty. If you think that only people with jobs and 401Ks can be fulfilled, look for the exceptions.

In order to get yourself unstuck you need to become your own good boss. If you are plagued by any of the following three, there is a good chance that you are stifling your own self and your own creativity, which you need to move forward. This is something most of us get conditioned to do over the course of our lives. Here are three exercises you can use to get yourself out from under your own thumb.

Exercise #16: Support all answers: There is a basic tenet behind becoming a more creative business: say "yes" before you say "no". Many people think the first step is engaging their logical mind and determining whether an idea is good or not, but the bottom line is that bad ideas are the fodder of really great ideas. When we get all the ideas out on the table, the options — and especially the good options — multiply exponentially. So brainstorm. What are all the potential solutions to your problem?

Exercise #17: Encourage involvement: Encouraging involvement means you are open to each and every person who is willing to put their two cents in. Why do you want to do this? Because this also helps your ideas become as powerful and innovative as possible. This does not mean you take every opinion at equal value; it means you engage as many people as possible and let this be the soup that ultimately creates your idea.

Exercise #18: Think outside of the box: When you do these first two things, you will set the stage for the third. The primary ingredient for creativity is being willing to look where no one has looked before. That is why it is so important to listen to everyone and to listen to all ideas. Wacky ideas are outside of the box and they help us find the good ideas that are also out there.

Exercise #19: On the other hand, if you are getting stuck when faced with a particular task, you can ask yourself some of the following questions to start to get unstuck:

1. What is the one thing I've been unwilling to do that I know is holding me back?

2. Is there an easier way to do it than I previously thought? It is really helpful to ask someone else if there is an easier way. Often times, there is a reason we have been unable to see the easier way and it is just faster to get help.

3. What action am I willing to commit to and when will I complete it? In other words, there is no time like the present. Find a good next step and put it in your schedule.

Although it may not always feel like it, staying put usually hurts more than moving forward. So take that step — one step closer to your fulfilled life — and take it as soon as possible.

Frequently, when people are unable to get at their Purpose, they start to look for flaws in themselves, others, or their project. They might think, "What is wrong with me?" Or, "Why is it every time I try to move forward I have problems with this person or that person?" Or, they think, "Is this even the right idea? Maybe I have been wrong about the idea from the beginning." Sometimes people can even miss everything that is going right because of the fact that they are looking at only part of the information — the negative part.

Abundance Mindset

Recognize the abundant nature of the universe and align yourself with it. Abundance is an essential part of being successful at living our life's Purpose. We cannot do our work without understanding how to make it work for us on all levels — including energetically and monetarily.

Very frequently, people put money between themselves and whatever it is they want to do. I am not going to tell you that money makes no difference. It does. Having the capital to develop your plan and take the action that needs to be taken makes some decisions — and even fulfilling your whole plan — much easier. However, don't be fooled into thinking money is the make-or-break factor in your plan. More often than not, passion and ingenuity can triumph over some of the most difficult situations. Sometimes, if you have a very large problem with money, you might even need to do some work around it before beginning work on your plan.

When what you are bringing into the world is needed, what is needed inevitably becomes available. This is true with money as well. Have faith that, if you begin to move in the direction of your ultimate goal, things will shift and the way will be clearer. Don't give up. However, please do not take that to mean that hard work is not necessary. Be prepared to do what it takes for something to which you are dedicated.

Exercise #20, Negative beliefs about money: Write down your negative beliefs about money. Then, rephrase these beliefs to be more positive — yet still believable. If you find you are particularly negative about money, you might want to write down your positive beliefs and reread them daily for a time. Without changing these beliefs, your chances at success will be limited. There is only so long that we can keep going without the resources we need to do so.

Abundance and prosperity are, of course, not just about money. It is an attitude — a belief that what is there in the moment is everything that needs to be there in the moment. It is the ability to see when things are out of balance and make course corrections that allow the situation to become healthier and more generative.

Exercise #21: Define abundance and prosperity for yourself. What does this look like for you? How would you know if you had it?

Leadership: The Key to Your Success

In this final section, I would like to leave you with some thoughts about leadership. Leadership is an essential component of our being able to live our Purpose in the world and, therefore, be deeply fulfilled. Leadership, and seeing ourselves as leaders, helps us recognize our impact with all we do. It helps us move — from a childlike perspective where we want the world to meet us and our needs — to an adult perspective where we want to meet the world. This is fundamental to our overall fulfillment and not something that many work to achieve.

From my own experience, I know it's easy to get stuck in the more childish part of myself that wants to be given to rather than to give. I can see this in relationships, in business, and even with myself. The part of us that just wants to take — that wants the world to meet us and give to us unconditionally and consistently — can only be satisfied when this is actually happening. This drastically limits our sense of fulfillment and effectiveness in creating a positive impact. We go along, looking to have our needs met in each and every situation and paying more attention to that than to what we are trying to create. In business, we might look at how people will serve our needs rather than how we can serve the bigger picture of everyone and everything that is involved.

As we move our Purpose into the world — or sometimes even before we get started — we might see that we are coming from a less than empowered place. Sometimes we might even start to feel uncomfortable with our conscious or semi-conscious Awareness of how we are approaching others. Maybe it is because, on some level, we know that it gets in the way of our bringing our Purpose out into the world. Here are three steps to help you make a perspective shift from disempowered to leader:

Exercise #22:

1. Ask yourself: "What do I want?" This allows you to become clear about what your needs are so you can be honest about how you are trying to gain them.

2. Ask yourself: "Does this work for everyone?" If not, who does it not work for and why does it not work for them?

3. Ask yourself: "Are there other ways I can do this that would serve the needs of more than just me?"

There are 15 key components of leadership, which I teach about in many of my programs.

15 Leadership Mastery Skills

1. Regular Practice/Reflection: Take time for spiritual practice, meditation, personal growth work, time with teachers and mentors.

2. Emotional Intelligence: Know what you are feeling when you are feeling it; know and understand the feelings of others.

3. Purpose: Know your deepest calling.

4. Balance Between Heart and Head: Remember that both thoughts and emotions are essential to the process and use the best tool for the job.

5. Abundance Mindset: Recognize the abundant nature of the universe and align yourself with it.

6. Communication: Learn how to speak, listen, and even argue effectively.

7. Networking: Understand the power of connecting with others and use it.

8. Empowering: Facilitate others living their deepest calling and standing in their full power.

9. Cultivating Brilliance: Welcome talented people and let them be experts at what they do best.

10. Sales and Marketing: Learn how to reach people and get them to say yes (when appropriate) to what you are offering.

11. Possibility and Opportunity: Facilitate the best possibility and learn to see the opportunities even in the problems.

12. Mastery: Strive to know everything about what you do and how to do it well.

13. Maximum Positive Effect: Learn how to make every action create a positive and transformational impact.

14. Vision: See the big picture and help others achieve it.

15. Inspiration: Help others feel hope and potential, stay motivated, and focused.

Exercise #23, Take stock: How many of these skills are you practicing in your life at this time?

Exercise #24, Rate yourself: Rate your ability on the scale of 0-10 (0 meaning not at all and 10 being mastery).

Exercise #25, What is important: Which of these skills do you feel are most important to living your life Purpose?

Exercise #26, Create a plan: What can you start doing or change in your life to move three of these leadership skills along?

Action-based Therapy

My dream is a world where we are not just doing therapy behind closed doors but, rather, it is woven into our lives in such a way that we are able to learn and grow through being of service to the world. This service begins to work on us — with the proper teaching — in much the same way washing the dishes at a Buddhist monastery might work for someone. We learn about ourselves by being in the world — not by being separate from it. We grow our potential simultaneously on the inside and outside through learning valuable lessons that immediately become a part of how we live.

If we wait until we are finished working on ourselvevs to begin making a difference in the world, we will lose precious time — we will never be finished developing ourselves. In most cases, we can start offering our service to the world much sooner than we expect. And when we do, we find that a sense of fulfillment keeps growing and growing in our lives. Every moment has the potential of healing and transformation.

I created my Mentoring program so people can get the real-time support and guidance they need — to provide support for their work in their daily life rather than behind office doors. Having a mentor is about living more fully. We need to pay attention to the parts of our life that need to be developed and have someone teach us the skills we need to move forward in the best possible way. It is true that, sometimes, we might need to work in the more conventional environment, but I think it is time to acknowledge the limit to the effectiveness of this method.

Exercise #27: Think how you can use your actions in the world to make a difference — both inside and out.

Remember to do something each day that continues to move forward you positive impact on the world. However we do it and whatever we do, you will see the profound impact it has on others and on your own sense of fulfillment.

Be inspirational!

CONCLUSION

Happiness is not a reward; it is a consequence. — *Robert Ingersoll*

We have gone through decades of New Age rhetoric, self-help, and the like. Our lives are only going to get better if we make an effort to make everyone's lives better. Our lives are only going to get better if we have the tools and encouragement to put in the effort. To do this, we need to become self-aware — to understand our impact, make efforts to see rather than negate our Connection to all things, and take action in the world in a way that makes a difference in our lives and the lives of others.

I have wondered, at times, what it is that pulls a person in this direction. I think there are many reasons. There is an unfolding in our lives that reaffirms the value of fulfilling our life's Purpose. We are drawn forward. We know that what we do matters. Once we realize this, we are never able to go back to thinking we are not leaving a mark on the world as a result of being here. Some of us are immediately called into the healing and helping professions, but soon find it is just the beginning of our work. We may discover through difficulty — such as burn-out or difficulty getting traction that we need to continue to reach toward fulfillment — that we require more information to develop ourselves and increase the potential of our work.

While this book has a lot of information, it only scratches the surface of the tools, techniques, and mindset we need to create a fulfilled life. When you are interested in moving forward, check the back of this book for resources.

I have had the pleasure of putting the ideas in this book into action for both myself and others — seeing the result of fostering an environment that helps people become more self-aware, more connected and more accustomed to empowered action. Each time I have done this, I have developed my skills as I helped others develop their skills. The effect has been profound — from the development of a center that is full of health and well-being and serves a multitude of clients, to meeting with women from a remote Mayan village to help them develop more sustainability and prosperity. Across the board, people respond by stepping in, getting things done, and creating healing.

Whether or not we ever have a chance to work together, I would like to say thank you. Thank you for putting your full self in. Thank you for putting in the effort to make a difference and to help others do the same.

RESOURCES

Programs with Dr. Kate

Awareness and Connection

- LifeWork 1 Mentoring
  http://www.lifefulfillmentformula.com/lifework1

- LifeWork 2 Retreats
  http://www.lifefulfillmentformula.com/lifework2

- LifeWork 3 Virtual
  http://www.lifefulfillmentformula.com/lifework3

Purpose

- Serious Success 1 Mentoring
  http://www.lifefulfillmentformula.com/serious-success1

- Serious Success 2 Mastermind
  http://www.lifefulfillmentformula.com/serious-success2

- Serious Success 3 Virtual
  http://www.lifefulfillmentformula.com/serious-success3

Classic Books & Audio CDs

Awareness

A Road Less Traveled **by M. Scott Peck**
Written in a voice that is timeless in its message of understanding, The
Road Less Traveled helps us explore the very nature of loving relationships

and leads us toward a new serenity and fullness of life. It helps us learn how to distinguish dependency from love; how to become a more sensitive parent; and ultimately how to become one's own true self.

Hands of Light **by Barbara Brennan**
With the clarity of a physicist and the compassion of a gifted healer with fifteen years of professional experience observing 5,000 clients and students, Barbara Ann Brennan presents the first in-depth study of the human energy field for people who seek happiness, health and their full potential.

Pathworks of Transformation **by Eva Pierrakos**
For more than twenty years, noted therapist Eva Pierrakos was the channel for a spirit entity known only as the Guide. Combining rare psychological depth and insight with an inspiring vision of human possibility, the Guide's teachings, known as the Pathwork, have influenced people all over the world.

The Power of Your Spoken Word **by Louise Hay**
On this engaging and spirited CD program, Louise helps you discover your own power, wisdom, and inner strength through the mastery of the words you speak.

Feel the Fear and Do It Anyway **by Susan Jeffers**
Are you afraid of making decisions… asking your boss for a raise… leaving an unfulfilling relationship… facing the future? Whatever your fear, here is your chance to push through it once and for all.   Dr. Susan Jeffers inspires us with dynamic techniques and profound concepts that have helped countless people grab hold of their fears and move forward with their lives.

The Buddha's Mind **by Rick Hanson**
The brain physiology associated with spiritual states has been fertile ground for researchers and writers alike. Neuropsychologist and meditation teacher Hanson suggests that an understanding of the brain in conjunction with 2,500-year-old Buddhist teachings can help readers achieve more happiness.

The Power of Now **by Eckhart Tolle**

Ekhart Tolle's message is simple: living in the now is the truest path to happiness and enlightenment. And while this message may not seem stunningly original or fresh, Tolle's clear writing, supportive voice, and enthusiasm make this an excellent manual for anyone who's ever wondered what exactly "living in the now" means.

Connection

Co-dependent No More **by Melody Beattie**

Is someone else's problem your problem? If, like so many others, you've lost sight of your own life in the drama of tending to someone else's, you may be codependent — and you may find yourself in this book.

People Skills **by Robert Bolton**

Author Robert Bolton describes the twelve most common communication barriers, showing how these "roadblocks" damage relationships by increasing defensiveness, aggressiveness, or dependency. He explains how to acquire the ability to listen, assert yourself, resolve conflicts, and work out problems with others. These are skills that will help you communicate calmly, even in stressful emotionally charged situations.

5 Languages of Love **by Gary Chapman**

"How do we meet each other's deep emotional need to feel loved? If we can learn that and choose to do it, then the love we share will be exciting beyond anything we ever felt when we were infatuated." — Dr. Gary Chapman

Non-Violent Communication: A Language of Life **by Marshall B. Rosenberg**

In this internationally acclaimed text, Marshall Rosenberg offers insightful stories, anecdotes, practical exercises and role-plays that will dramatically change your approach to communication for the better.

The Mastery of Love **by Miguel Ruiz**

In a refreshingly honest investigation of the true nature of love, don Miguel Ruiz brings to light the commonly held fallacies and misplaced expectations about love that permeate most relationships.

Difficult Conversations **by Douglas Stone, Bruce Patton & Shelia Heen**
We attempt or avoid difficult conversations every day-whether dealing with an underperforming employee, disagreeing with a spouse, or negotiating with a client. From the Harvard Negotiation Project, the organization that brought you Getting to Yes, Difficult Conversations provides a step-by-step approach to having those tough conversations with less stress and more success.

Getting the Love You Want **by Harville Hendrix**
Originally published in 1988, Getting the Love You Want has helped millions of couples attain more loving, supportive, and deeply satisfying relationships.

Action

Get Out Of Your Own Way! **by Larry Winget**
In this perspective-altering program, Larry Winget, exposes the things you are doing right now to unknowingly prevent your own success in the most important areas of your life: business, family, health, parenting, money and more - and offers you his self-proven action plan for change.

Rich Dad, Poor Dad **by Rober Kiyosaki**
Anyone stuck in the rat-race of living paycheck to paycheck, enslaved by the house mortgage and bills, will appreciate this breath of fresh air. Learn about the methods that have created more than a few millionaires.

Think and Grow Rich **by Napoleon Hill**
Napoleon Hill's classic mental-exercise book teaches you everything you need to know to empower yourself for success. Drawing on the experiences of not only the author, but famous U.S. businessmen, Hill makes real-world lessons which anyone can follow.

As a Man Thinketh **by James Allen**
"As a Man Thinketh" is a literary essay by James Allen, first published in 1902. In more than a century it has become an inspirational classic, selling millions of copies worldwide and bringing faith, inspiration, and self healing to all who have encountered it.

7 Habits of Highly Effective People **by Stephen Covey**

Full of advice on taking control of your life, teamwork, self-renewal, mutual benefit, proactivity, and other paths to private and public victory.

How to Win Friends and Influence People **by Dale Carnegie**

Fundamental techniques in handling people and winning people to your way of thinking without arousing resentment.

A New Earth **by Echart Tolle**

Tolle describes how our attachment to the ego creates the dysfunction that leads to anger, jealousy, and unhappiness, and shows readers how to awaken to a new state of consciousness and follow the path to a truly fulfilling existence.

Getting Things Done **by David Allen**

Allen's premise is simple: our productivity is directly proportional to our ability to relax. Only when our minds are clear and our thoughts are organized can we achieve effective productivity and unleash our creative potential.

How Remarkable Women Lead **by Joanna Barsh, Susie Cranston & Geoffrey Lewis**

It's the new "right stuff" of leadership, raising provocative issues such as whether feminine leadership traits (for women and men) are better suited for our fast-changing, hyper-competitive, and increasingly complex world.

Featured Resources

Rissa Sullivan

Discover your own path and how to navigate your inner truth. Rissa works to uncover the knowledge and confidence hidden with in you. Her tools of Practical Spiritual Development clear away blocks and negative energies carried from others. You will be left with strength and the assurance you can make sound choices for your own personal truth.

Rissa has been working with people on a spiritual level for over 10 years. She has the unique ability to see within a person past the masks we where. During your work with her you will have personal plans for moving energy, developing new patterns to move you to your goals.

Rissa works with clients in person in the New England area as well as distance.

Rissa Sullivan
http://www.rissasullivan.com

Ann Bennett

Ann Bennett is a speaker, author, coach and creator of her 7 Step Irresistible Marketing and Mindset System. Ann uses her marketing and banding genius along with her high content high value coaching programs to help women entrepreneurs make significant six-figure incomes. Ann's personal slogan, the corner stone of all her programs, is to be audaciously bold and authentically unique; "It's smart to fit in... but it's Brilliant to stand out".

Ann Bennett Marketing
http://www.annbennettmarketing.com
ann@annbennettmarketing.com
(949) 287-6410

Emily J. Volden, LICSW

Does your life feel frenzied, scattered, or disorganized and leaves you questioning your ability to ever make gains in developing your goals, dreams, or greatest desires? Are you so overwhelmed by managing daily responsibilities that you lack the time or energy to enjoy your favorite activities and relationships?

If this sounds like you, Emily J. Volden's ADHD Aptitude programs may be the solution you have been looking for. The programs are designed to help you gain the skills and strategies needed to navigate your daily personal and professional responsibilities with ease, while creating and sustaining the highest quality of life.

We live in a world that is fast-paced, highly competitive, and screaming for our attention. ADHD minds — creative, action-oriented, and flexible — naturally respond with a sense of urgency, seeking better, faster, and more innovative ways to perform. At one point or another, that which was once energizing to us becomes draining and insurmountable. We get overwhelmed. We feel scattered. Our stress levels rise. We try to give it our all, but rarely feel like our efforts are ever enough.

Through integrative psychotherapy, solution-focused coaching, and educational offerings, Emily Volden mindfully inspires and empowers individuals, couples, and organizations impacted by ADHD to realize effective solutions to life's challenges and stimulate positive transformation. The programs she offers ensure that you will get the help you need with focus, organization, decision making, time management, relationships, communication, frustration tolerance, impulse control, and much more. Explore the impact Emily and her ADHD Aptitude programs can have on your life at:

ADHD Aptitude
http://www.adhdaptitude.com

ALisa Starkweather

ALisa Starkweather is an outstanding visionary and transformational leader whose expertise since 1984 is women's empowerment. Known for her soulful personal-growth containers, she masterfully facilitates facing one's inner saboteurs, resistance patterns and shadows, in unique ways. People experience large shifts from many of her modalities including archetypal symbolism, Shadow Work™, skill building and reclamation. ALisa is opening her schedule to include Transformational Breakthrough VIP sessions for private clients who apply.

ALisa shows women how to pull aside the veil to access our own inner potential and live our highest Purpose. C.M

ALisa is the founder of the Red Tent Temple Movement, Daughters of the Earth Gatherings, Women's Belly and Womb Conferences and co-founder of Women in Power; Initiating Ourselves to the Predator Within, a global initiation. She also runs a two year intensive which spans over thirteen weekends with women from the US, Canada and Europe. She is the co-producer of the film, Things We Don't Talk About; Healing Stories from the Red Tent and is published author in the award winning anthology, Women, Spirituality, and Transformative Leadership; Where Grace Meets

Power. ALisa has recorded two online courses, Answering the Call; Birthing Your Fierce Feminine Self and Shadow Work Archetypes Toolbox; Forging Powerful Partnerships from Within.

ALisa facilitates a shifting within the core of being to a more honest, powerful, raw, courageous, luscious woman to all she touches. M.L.

ALisa Starkweather
http://www.alisastarkweather.com
She Loves Life
PO Box 13
Baldwinville, MA 01436

WORDS OF PRAISE

Are you ready to stop doing what you have always done and make a REAL shift in your life? Dr. Kate gives you step by step guidance to create lasting change in your life... which will have you living a life of greater fulfillment, Purpose and joy.

— Belinda Pruyne, Business Innovation Group
http://www.businessinnovationgroup.com

Kate ROCKS! She is a true visionary with the skills of an effective, clean communicator. She's recognized the shift that is happening in the world with more women stepping up as leaders. She has created a comprehensive program to really propel that shift.

Prior to working with Kate, I had familiarity and even experience with various leadership styles and group dynamics, but they did not have names and labels. The labels are not important in and of themselves but now I recognize that they are actually identifiable components that I can watch for instead of intuiting. That alone has expanded my Awareness and increased my confidence in my leadership abilities.

The bottom line is that I trust myself more and I recognize that I have something to offer!
— GK

I left each weekend saying to myself, "Wow, that was phenomenal!" I learned the pragmatics of leadership. I was given permission to learn how to be a leader which is different than how I have traditionally been taught. In my native culture, I am expected to learn through observation, by trial and error, and through really hard obstacles — always my integrity and resilience was tested or my ego. Through this program, I have learned a myriad of leadership modalities. I learned without ever being ashamed of my perceptions, thoughts, and ideas, and the culture from which I come. After this program I feel that I know in my gut that I

have the foundational/concrete skills to be a leader and to use my personal power for whatever change I wish to see in the world.
— LE

Before I started the working with Kate, I had visions and ideas but felt overwhelmed by the magnitude of them. I was convinced I did not have the tools, energy, skills, charisma to manifest these visions. The three most significant things that I learned from Kate are. 1.) The only thing standing between me and my visions is my fear. 2.) All my excuses are just old tapes and I have the ability to change them. 3.) I have a much better understanding of how groups work, how to keep a group together, functional, and worthy of everyone's time.
— KG

I entered this program wanting to learn more about myself and how to be a better facilitator, organizer, and leader in my own life and in my community. There was a huge sense of knowing that my soul's passion wants to come forth, and urgency, and a desire to better understand what I am trying to create in the world. I knew where I wanted to end up but not how to get there.

Through this program, I have learned so many valuable listening skills that come in handy daily and enrich my interactions with others. I discovered a leadership style that is unique, empowering to myself and to others and breaks the paradigm of what I thought in the past was "the only way to make it work." I have embraced and learned to really understand a more feminine, strong, and inspiring way to move forward in the world — available to all of us.

This program also provided me with access to amazing resources and wonderful guest teachers who fueled my hunger to learn more and more

and to continue working and striving to understand more about how women are leading change and what a difference we are making.
— TG

Kate is an amazing leader and teacher. I am so grateful I was able to take part in this program. I am leaving, not only with new leadership skills but with a renewed and heightened sense of self. I am able to identify what kind of leader I am, where my strengths are and also what I'd like to improve. I can't think of a more skilled, compassionate, and intelligent person to lead a program like this. Kate leads with integrity and grace. Kate is great!

Specifically, I came out of this program with a better sense of who I am as a leader. What gifts I have to give are now known to me. I also gained an expansion of my knowledge about tools I can use as a leader to lead in a holistic way.
— KN

For me, this program set my feet squarely on the path to share my gifts with the world, and stop stalling or sidestepping my highest vision for my life... no more excuses for not having the life I want and living from some place other than my creativity and passion. It surprised me how clearly things snapped into focus through the individual and group work we did. Kate guided us more deeply into Awareness and consciousness of ourselves while quickly creating a safe space for the journey, internally and within the group of women. We reflected on the group's work and growth as a team, and the experience of being the living model for the progress we were learning about made many of the teachings experiential, which I loved.

Since teaching is part of my vision for my life, the pieces that Kate modeled as facilitator about sharing power, being vulnerable, being 'in the mess', authentic and present, and shifting group energy and dynamics have taken me into a place where I am comfortable in this role, and can see the richness to be harvested from some places I would have avoided prior to this program. This program exposes the wisdom we hold that we miss because we're so used to ourselves, and offers skills to facilitate and navigate where we have not yet gained experience. It is empowering to stand in each moment fearlessly sharing your gifts with the world, and that is exactly what Kate is doing, and what she is offering to the women who go through this program.

— AC

Kate Siner Francis, Ph.D. teaches an experience of and model for the change I wish to see in the world. The program far exceeded my expectations and cultivated strength, confidence, Connection, and direction in my leadership. Before participating in the program, I was an active leader in a variety of professional roles; however, I struggled with committing to a project or collaborative venture and seeing it through to its completion, staying organized and accountable, identifying and trusting my strengths, and asking for help or support when it was needed. Throughout the 6 month process, both Kate and the group participants helped me to identify and transform the underlying beliefs and limiting behaviors that were blocking me from practicing effective leadership. This program inspired me to step into my Purpose in the world, to identify my vision and goals, to learn experientially about myself as a leader, and most importantly, to trust my leadership abilities. Kate's facilitation style and educational approach promotes a wealth of learning around the foundations of leadership by helping participants to develop an understanding of effective collaboration, communication, decision-making, and approach to leadership. The diversity of experience, specialties, and vision among the group as well as the common denominator of commitment and desire for change fosters a dimension of personal and professional growth that is indescribable... unlike anything I have ever experienced! It is without reservation that I recommend this program to any woman who has a deep seated

commitment to something larger than herself and a hunger for more conceptual and personal tools with which to practice.

— EV

Congratulations! You bought the book
and now you're moving forward to...

Live Your Greatest Life!

To support you in living a deeply Fulfilled Life,
I have a Special FREE gift for you!

Join me online for this one-time offer:
www.LifeFulfillmentFormula.com/free-gift

with Dr. Kate Siner

Visit my website to get your free gift now!

Psychologist, speaker, writer and educator, Kate Siner PhD has been called "a rock star of the soul." As a true visionary and critically acclaimed public speaker, Kate advocates for a much needed shift in our world today.

ABOUT THE AUTHOR

Kate Siner, Ph.D.

Psychologist, speaker, writer and educator Dr. Kate has been called a true visionary. As a professional speaker Dr. Kate advocates for a much needed shift in the world today. She has dedicated her career to helping people find and develop their own fulfillment and success by connecting to their true selves and taking powerful action.

Dr. Kate provides world-class training in entrepreneurial and personal development for value-driven entrepreneurs and individuals who want to build a generative, highly profitable business that has a positive impact on the world as well as leads to a fulfilled life. Dr. Kate's clients come from around the world to get the training they need to be as successful and impactful as they were born to be.

Kate Siner Inc.
150 Waterman St. #G
Providence, RI 02906
http://www.lifefulfillmentformula.com
admin@lifefulfillmentformula.com
(401) 272-4578

21771900R00069

Made in the USA
Lexington, KY
28 March 2013